The Nature of Bastard

When A Son Forfeits His Inheritance!

Lay Hands On No Man Suddenly!

Cover & Graphic Design by Jeremiah Silva

Kingdom Empowerment Network Group

Publisher:

P.O. Box 3002 Springfield, IL 62708

Library of Congress Control Number: TXu 1-843-082

ISBN10: 0981976913

ISBN-13:978-0-9819769-1-4

ACKNOWLEDGEMENTS

The book entitled, "The Nature of a Bastard When A Son Has Forfeited His Inheritance!" written by Dr. Kenneth D. Grimble is very sincere and insightful. I like what I read and feel the enlightenment in which you have presented. These truths you have written about in this book qualify to help perfect the body of Christ today.

Apostle Cletus C. Doss
Love Deliverance Evangelistic Church
Springfield, IL

The book entitled, "The Nature of a Bastard When A Son Has Forfeited His Inheritance" is a thoroughly put together masterpiece which I believe should be added to everyone's ministry library. This book written by Dr. Kenneth D. Grimble is very challenging and thought-provoking. Definitely a must read. I recommend this literary piece to the entire body of Christ everywhere.

Apostle Christopher L. McCarter
Kingdom Destiny Deliverance Center UCOGIC
East Hartford, CT

The book entitled, "The Nature of A Bastard When A Son Has Forfeited His Inheritance!" is an awesome read and a wonderful contribution to the body of Christ. This book is a timely read and one that I truly enjoyed. This book is filled with truths and nuggets that have been hidden until now. Dr. Kenneth D. Grimble has been used by God to bring forth his revealed truth. Continue to write man of God and allow God to use you as the ready pen writer.

Bishop Dr. Ellen S. Jones
Memphis, TN

ENDORSEMENTS

The book entitled, "The Nature of a Bastard When A Son Has Forfeited His Inheritance!" is a must read for the body of Christ. I am truly in awe at the prowess Archbishop Kenneth D. Grimble in terms of how he captured the heart of God in this writing. It felt like I was sitting at God's feet listening to him read an instruction book on what he expects his people to look like. The vision for the sublime revelation of the scriptures, as it defines son-ship, has been clarified for God's people in this masterpiece. Archbishop Kenneth Grimble have touched on subjects that are not only experienced by mankind in general but which continue to be a stumbling block for the church in particular. Your insights on marriage, family, prayer and church authority are not only relevant but absolutely necessary for true spiritual authority. I felt that Archbishop Kenneth Grimble uncovered truths that have been touched on only superficially in the church of today when they should be shouted from the rooftops in order for God's people to take their true role in society. Sobering, convicting, corrective and timely are the words that come to mind in describing this book and I wait in eager expectation to read your next one!

Sarah Newton
Reimage Church
Winterville, NC

The book entitled, "The Nature of A Bastard When A Son Forfeits His Inheritance!" is not only a timely message to the body of Christ, but is a subject close to my heart. Having dealt with both true sons and bastard sons, and in the process of completing my own book on this subject. My hat goes off to you Dr. Grimble and thank you for the honor of reading this your manuscript. When I think how you broke down not only the spiritual but natural aspects of sonship and the nature of fatherhood. When you refer to the Patriarchs of scripture ie, Abraham, Solomon and how we have laid the foundation for children of disobedience to show up in our lives. As the Patriarch of an International Ministry and Spiritual Father to thousands, I have given Dr. Kenneth Grimble my full support and endorsement of this book, and we will add it to our school as required reading.

++++Archbishop Dr. Charles R. Hill Sr.
Patriarch and Visionary of Ambassador For Christ Ministries of America

DEDICATION

I want to dedicate this book to first and foremost to my wife and partner in faith Lady Diane Grimble. She believed in me and stuck by my side when I know that she should have taken the first flight out. My wife has been a source of strength that propelled me to push when everything in me said to give up and quit.

Lady Diane Grimble, I not only dedicate this book to you but also I also dedicate my life to you.......you are a wonderful friend, drill instructor, lover, wife and leader in the Kingdom of our Lord God.

I also dedicate this book to my mother, the late Bessie N. Grimble who was a pillar of strength, wisdom, knowledge and kindness in all the days of her life.

I dedicate this book to my father, Herb, brother, Kelvin, aunt, Jennie, my mother-in-law, Juanita.

I dedicate this book to my daughter Amber, two sons Antawn & Marvel.

I dedicate this book to my cousins Ricky, Harold, Lamont, Jeff, Felicia, Keisha...(too many to list).

I dedicate this book to my spiritual sons and daughters.

I dedicate this book to my spiritual father Archbishop Willie Bolden.

I dedicate this book to my spiritual mother, Apostle Dr. Polly Elliot.

I dedicate this book to my friends, associates and my enemies dedicate this book to all my professors, instructors and teachers and spiritual leaders.
Each member of my family that have played a role in my development as a Man of God that I became today.

I also want to say to my Grand Children, Ashton and Addison, you are a source of Joy and delight to me, Grand Daddy Loves you dearly.

CONTENTS

PREFACE

The legacy of leaving an inheritance for the next generation have been imposed for centuries. A real man would prepare his life so that he could leave something for the next generation. The process of preparing for the inheritance has been somewhat sluggish or lethargic because so many men in the African American communities did not have fair access to provisions for their families. With efforts that were designed to destroy the black man or demoralize him to the point that he could not take care of his family is a major program in society. Unfortunately, the cycle pushed some men into the extent of abandoning their responsibilities and living a life on the streets because they could not support them. The shame of this plight and a strategic effort to demoralize this man to ostracize himself from his family. Although the African American man was not the only pawn in this game of life illustrated by capitalist society. Other races and some poor

11

Caucasians were also victims. This book is not an issue on race or racism but we mention in because it was a part of the problem. In Luke 12:13-21 Jesus downplays the importance of an earthly inheritance, explaining that I could lead to greed and an obsession with wealth. He emphasized that it was far better to store up treasures in heaven. Parents are always concerned for the welfare of their children and prepare to leave them provisions once they depart from this world. This same mode of preparation should be employed by the children as they mature into adulthood. They should also follow the same plans and activities for their children.

INTRODUCTION

The spurious nature of mankind have always been plagued with slight tinge of rebellion. Even though good will always outweigh evil, there is a strong propensity for warfare between good and evil. God has given every free will moral agent the propensity to do good. However, the pull to do wrong is forever present. According to Romans 7: 19, the bible says, "For the good that I would I do not: but the evil which I would not, that I do." Apostle Paul clearly states that in the above text that every time I attempt to do something but I do not. However, the evil that lingers around me and I know not to do I end up doing . From the last chapter and last verse in the book of Malachi, we read the latter text that informs fathers and sons that they must deal with some issues. God had so graciously given both fathers and sons a commandment to have a heart transformation but they chose to disregard this mandate. Nevertheless, the consequence of not following orders has brought us into a reality check that God has levied a curse. The reaction to the curse has now placed us in realm of our archenemy in the devil. Because of disobedience and failure to follow instructions, we have seen a continuous plague of sin. The sin continuous to tear up families because no one honors the institution of marriage. In the days of old, it would be shame to bring a child in this world without being married. The influx of promiscuity along with an extremely high rate of pregnancy among teenager. Unfortunately, the birth rate of babies are coming at an alarming rate.

The after effect of this pattern of reproduction continues to bring children into this world with no understanding that their children are illegitimate. When a child carries the stigma of illegitimacy, there is a negative association to the child that implies they are contagious or unworthy. The cycle is promulgated by those who continue to live in sin and realize that their child has no legitimacy. Even when the father is in the child's life, the child loses his or her authenticity because he does not have a birth rite through marriage. The stigma of being a bastard has caused many children to feel unworthy, unwanted and undeserving of real undaunted love. This same pattern has spilled over into the churches. The leaders in the churches have abandoned the thought of the welfare of their spiritual children to seek after fame, wealth and notoriety.

CHAPTER 1
FORWARD PROGRESS

The shame of failure has prevented so many who claim to know God intimately from moving into a progressive relationship with him. Although the inhabitants of the past were too busy to Worship God, they were benefactors of his grace and mercy. Yet, serving other gods seemed to be a great conduit because it appeased and gratified their flesh. This nature of the flesh is rotten to the core and does not want to abandon any ground to our creator. Evil has been in competition with God since the eons of time. It appears in another dimension where the creature is competing with his creator.

Because God created evil to be a part of his balanced scale, Lucifer felt a need to try to take authority from God. The plot thickens with the devil as he continues to unmask his task as a King of Darkness and prince of certain atmospheric levels. He was given the ability to transform himself into the angel of light. God granted his darkness a kingdom after all, for trying his futile attempts to over throw the King of Kings, the Lord of Lords and the God of Gods. With power beyond measure, it is amazing that the devil would make such a powerless move. This is not the same as someone trying to take over a business by purchasing all outstanding stock. On the contrary, this thee ultimate power source, with unlimited resources and power that the devil thought he could undermine.

It would appear that mediocrity had set in and the desire to move forward had dissipated. When a mountain climber sets out on a mission to climb the mountain, the intent is to start at the bottom to reach the top. The problem occurs in the pursuit of climbing where climbers decide that they no longer desires to go up but they don't want to go down either. The problems incurred are serious factors that can cause the human endeavors to be altered. For instance, it takes a great deal of endurance and coordination to pull and walk up a mountain. The physical conditioning and strength are major factors when considering such an arduous endeavor.

The lack of proper conditioning can be a deterrent for an endeavor of this magnitude. When feelings and determination cross the lines, there is a strong possibility that the desire to go to the top diminishes and the desire to return to the bottom dissipates. This is a great example of mediocrity.

When mediocrity sets in, the practitioners become immobile like a still born baby. The notion that an active vibrant individual loses the desire to move is extremely perplexing. The Old Testament and new testament of the bible give great examples of people who witness the miraculous powers of God, but refused to submit to his entire will.

One could easily surmise that the creator and creature had come to a cross roads. On one hand, there has always been a remnant of believers plucking away at the plan and will of God. Religion has always given the Christ followers, the 70 disciples, and an illusion of following the plan but there was no real connection to the power source. In so many words, there have always been witnesses of the power of God and some who just love the nature of sin. The delirious notion is that so many cannot tell the difference between their right and left hand. A lamb and the fall off disciples are very similar in that they have a similar pattern of thinking as they prepare for the great slaughter.

Moreover, the inhabitants under the religious pretense will never embark upon a genuine relationship because of a mind conditioned by erroneous information and poor teaching of mankind. The abdication from the Malachi Mandate is primarily one of the main reasons that a curse has been levied on society. In essence, the church has been stagnant in its efforts to become the manifested sons of God. According to Malachi 4:6 the writer says, "And he shall turn the heart of the fathers to the children, and the heart of the children to their fathers, lest I come and smite the earth with a curse. Let us zoom in on the latter part of the text.

The writer in which God spoke through prophet Malachi gives us a warning indicating that if the condition he dictated did not come to pass that God would come and smite the earth with a curse. Beloved, I submit to you that a curse has been levied on the earth. The chronological reason is the core of sin but most importantly is the blatant disrespect of Gods command to the fathers and sons. Historically, the fathers did not spend a great deal of time with their children due to the demand of their time in working and taking care of securing finances for household. While the Mothers were the foundation layers in terms of daily nurturing needs, the children lack the quality needed to give them balance.

The women not only worked in the garden while the men were out hunting for meat for the home and bartering rights to secure other household needs. The church is considered the mother and those of us who claim to be apart it don't have time to commune with the father. The father seeks to commune with his creation but the creation does not have time for the father. The lack of communion keeps the flesh from dying so that

21

the spirit man can become alive. As in the natural, so is it in the spirit. The churches are so temporal today in that they lack the very substance would eradicate all the sin that continues to parade in and out.

The missing substance that has being on a hiatus is the pure unadulterated power of God. In order for the church to regain the authority of God in the present tense, it is the need for a clarion call for prayer. Prayer is the very vehicle that is used to bring the creation into presence of the creator. God so richly loves us but has been denied the very essence of time speak with his creation. Furthermore, the creation does not make strides to walk in the type of relationship that would move God for us. The central fact of the matter is that mankind does not understand the nature of prayer and the power that comes from time spent with God. The saints of God needs to redevelop a love for God and fell the need to spend time in his presence so that he can get the time he desire for us.

Progress begins when his creation falls on their knees or lay prostrate on the ground and cry loud and spare not. God wants that quality time that is needed for a creator to supp with his creation. There is truly a need to reclaim what has been lost and redeem the time that has been. Dominion is a provision given by God to every person who has been born again. Because each born again member are now part of his family, God has made us kings and priest unto himself. Furthermore, God has made us to have dominion over the works of His hands. As we examine our roles as Kings and Priest, we must also understand that He made us Kings.

What do Kings do? They reign over and rule their kingdom. Moreover, we need to find out what the meaning of the words reign and dominion. The original Hebrew word for dominion is "radah" which means literally to rule over with Authority, to subjugate, the Right and the Power to Govern and Control, and to Dominate. Another word used for dominion in Psalms 8:6 is the word "mashal" which means to have ruling power over, to dominate and to make to have the right and power to govern or control. The original Greek word for Reign is the word "basileuo" which means literally to rule over with authority.

In Romans 8:17 the bible says," For if by one man's offence death reigned by one; much more they which receive abundance of grace and of the gift of righteousness shall reign in life by one, Jesus Christ.

CHAPTER 2
WHEN EVIL IS CONSIDERED GOOD?

The bible says in Isaiah 5:20,"Woe unto them that call evil good and good evil; that put darkness for light, and light for darkness; that put bitter for sweet and sweet for bitter!" There is a boldness of sinners that choose to invite God to hasten his threatened judgment that they might see it, and let His counsel come quickly that they might know it. This is the spirit of men who are totally abandoned to evil. Their conscience is seared as with a hot iron, and they are hardened through the deceitfulness of sin to the point of no concern whatsoever. Solomon, the son of King David, was touted as one of the wisest men of all time.

According to I Kings 3:5-9 the bible says, "In Gibeon the Lord appeared unto Solomon in a dream by night: and God said, Ask what I shall give the. And Solomon said, Thou hast shewed unto thy servant David my father great mercy, according as walked before the in truth, and in righteousness, and in uprightness of heart with the; and thou hast kept for him this great kindness, thou hast given him a son to sit on his throne, as it is this day. And now, O LORD my God, thou hast made thy servant king instead of David my father; and I am but a little child: I know not how to go out or come in. And thy servant is in the midst of thy people whom thou hast chosen, a great people that cannot be numbered nor counted for multitude. Give therefore thy servant an understanding heart to judge thy people, which I may discern between good and bad: for who is able to judge this thy so great a people?"

And the speech pleased the Lord, that Solomon had asked this thing. And God said unto him, Because thou hast asked this thing and hast not asked for thyself long life; neither has asked riches for thyself, nor hast asked life or thine enemies; but hast asked for thyself understanding to discern judgment; Behold, I have done according to thy words: lo, I have given thee a wise and an understanding heart; so that there was none like thee before thee neither after the shall any arise like unto thee." The early portion of Solomon's reign would epitomize an extremely close walk with God. In his petition to the father, he recalled all that God had done for his father David. King Solomon was aware that his father lived according to his word and he kept an upright heart. According to Deuteronomy 17:17 the bible says, "Neither shall he multiply wives to himself that his heart turns not away: neither shall he greatly multiply to himself silver and gold." The essence of this scripture implies that no one should have multiple wives nor should they have an excessive multiplicity of wealth.

The word here does not imply that wealth or marriage is a bad thing. It only implies when greed sets in for an excessive amount of wealth and wives would enable his focus to be taken off of God. The key word in the above mention statement is multiple wives. The inquiry now comes to fruition as to what is considered multiple wives. Numerically speaking, one would have to construe than any number above one.   Wealth, Women and Weaponry have the propensity to cause a person to take their focus off of the will of God and refocus on another type of God which is the God of mammon. It is apparent that Solomon took his eyes off of God in order to pursue the desires of his heart. This form of seduction and lust for wealth, women & weaponry is a plight that most men succumb.

Solomon used his quest for strange women as a means to seal a business deal. Therefore, each deal he sealed included a contingency that indicated as a signet is placed on the contract, the counterpart would include one of ungodly kings daughters would become part of his harem of wives. In other words, Kingdom Solomon aggressive pursuit for women and wealth propelled him to spread the gap between his relationship with God. According to scripture, Solomon used the institution of marriage to enhance his wealth and harem. It has been suggested that 700 wives and 300 concubines reported is an exaggeration. However, we shall stand by this because it is recorded in scripture. With this in mind, every man who hears this story ponders on the notion that they would like to switch places with Solomon. King Solomon became known in a case where a two women quarreled over the rights to a baby.

So, Solomon suggested that they split the baby in half and share equal parts of the baby. The real mother cried out and begged that the baby be given to the other woman. It was at this moment that Solomon could identify the real mother. The rumors of Solomon's wisdom had spread throughout the territory so much so that Queen Sheba had to pay him a visit.   The queen was amazingly surprised at what she witnessed through conversation so much that it exceeded her wildest imagination.   Solomon's wisdom and prosperity exceeded the fame in which she had heard. Furthermore, the queen was speechless at the cordial & respectful treatment that Solomon had given her. She was impressed by his regal surroundings and artistic effects of tables of gold, silver and glass. The queen had blessed him with several gifts that included gold, jewels, spices and precious stones. Solomon, on the other hand, was equally astonished with her conversation and dialogue about business and governmental issues she was seeking for her own kingdom.

Despite the wonderful accolades that King Solomon had experienced and achieved, he failed miserably in eyes of the Lord. He continued to walk in delusion as he had been warned about marrying strange women and the pursuit of excess wealth. Kingdom Solomon continued back sliding while displaying his wonderful gift of wisdom. The point of clarity is to determine if Solomon was operating with his own wisdom or the wisdom of the Lord. Depending on the way you access the way the Holy Spirit ascended, it appear that his heart had turned away from God entirely. There is a great supposition involved in the number of wives that a king was allowed. As the scriptures indicate to multiply, there would need to be only one.

However, there are scriptures that imply otherwise. Whereas King David has at least 7 wives and Kingdom Solomon 700, there has to be an answer as to why God favored these men so highly. In spite of the perception to appear that they have violated the marriage covenant, it is also apparent that God honored and favored both of them highly. Whether polygamy was prevalent or not in certain sects of society, it is clear that Gods intent was for marriage to be a monogamous relationship. Could it be the Judgment came on both King David and Solomon as a result of their bout with multiple wives. Now there is speculation in the Jewish tradition that kings were a loud to have up to 18 wives. Warning was given about multiple marriage and a particular emphasis was on being married to strange wives.

Some would argue that the focus was on strange wives not the multiple wives. On the contrary, the word of God has been spoken and it is clear that married was, is and has been identified by God has having one wife and one husband. The pattern of multiple marriages is treated as a luxury among those who don't identify the creator as the God of God and King of Kings. It is clear that these practitioners find it fitting to have multiple wives based on cultural factors and not based only on the word of God. There are those who know the context in which the scripture has been written but will play word games as to how to make it imply something else.   Proverbs 3:5 says, "Trust in the Lord with all your heart and lean not to your own understanding." The major emphasis here is lean not to your own understanding. This is the area where the creature is trying to get into a mind battle with the creator.

The wisdom of man has always felt a need to be equal with God. The fact of the matter is that a finite mind of the creature can not compare to an infinite mind of the creator. The believer, on the other hand, needs to connect with God on spiritual basis and make the initial effort to develop a pure relationship. The gathering of cosmic believers are identified and the body of Christ.   On the Contrary, hell is likened to the great whore in is reference to those non-believers in righteousness. The bible says in Hebrew 13:4," Marriage is honorable in all, and the bed undefiled: but whoremongers and adulteress God will judge. As a point of reference, Solomon and David had multiple wives. The potential have children was pre-eminent as engaged in marital relations. But if these marriages were not recognized by God, Solomon and David would have be consider a whoremonger and an adultery.   The children would be considered bastard because they were not conceived in a legitimate marriage.

Despite of the appearance of inappropriate actions of David and Solomon, it does not appear that either had a reproach against God for having multiple wives. It appears that the central focus is on the strange wives. Isaiah 4:1 And in that day, seven women shall take hold of one man say, We will eat our own bread, and wear our own apparel: only let us be called by thy name, to take away our reproach. The seven women in the above mentioned text is indicative of the scarcity of men after the tribulation and the battle of Armageddon. It is reported that there will not be enough men for the women to marry. This is one of the scriptures whereby men will use to justify a life of polygamy. Although some cultures have embraced this act, there are not scriptures that support the notion that man can have multiple wives.

Moreover, there is evidence that several keys person in the bible had more than one wife. Judges 5:30 says, "Have they not sped? Have they not divided the prey; to every man a damsel or two; to Sisera a prey of divers colours of needlework, on both sides, meet for the necks of them that take spoil. The concubine was an enslaved women from the spoil who dedicated herself to a particular man, with whom she cohabits without being marriage. This would be characterized as a live in girl friend but there was a wife in the same household. The concubine would advance in rank if she had a child for her man if the wife was barren. Generally speaking, only men of high social status could afford to have a concubine as a part of his harem. This arrangement was promulgated by the woman or a family arrangement, as it provides a measure of economic security for the women involved.

Genesis 25:5-6 says And Abraham gave all that he had unto Isaac, But unto the sons of the Concubines, which Abraham had, Abraham gave gifts, and sent them away from Isaac his son while he yet lived, eastward, unto the east country. In this case, the child is considered illegitimate because it was not born under the auspices of marriage. The sole purpose of concubines were to be a type of bond slave that aided in the household work force and provided sexual favors usually when the wife was barren. The children would be the property of the wife but they were not considered legitimate. In 2 Samuel 16:21-23, the bible says, "And Ahithophel said to Absalom, "Go in to your father's concubine, whom he has left to keep the house; and all Israel will hear that thou are abhorred of thy father: then shall the hands of all that are with thee be strong." So they spread a tent for Absalom upon the top of the house, and Absalom went in to his father's concubines in the sight of all Israel.

And the counsel of Ahithophel which he counseled in those days, was as if a man had inquired at the oracle of God so was all the counsel of Ahithophel both with David and with Absolam" The lewdness of sexuality was spearheaded from such patterns poorly established by predecessors. Judges 8:30 says," And Gideon had threescore and ten sons of his body begotten: for he had many wives. And his concubine that was in Shechem, she also bore him a son, and called his name Abimeliech.

CHAPTER 3
AN EXPOSE OF SONSHIP

The great debate about the mature and immature nature of son-ship and the efforts to get an understanding of the essence of son-ship has been perplexing. From both the natural and spiritual aspect of son-ship, there is an urgent need for an awakening to this arena. The social spectrum would indicate that we are losing our men either to death, prison or debilitating diseases. The cry for sons to be affirmed by their parents is an amazing experience. Because of the alarming divorce rate, the after affects of the children have been hit like a hurricane. Many of the children are left thinking that they played a part in the divorce. On the spiritual side, divorce has also made an impact because you now have to make a choice which one of the leaders are we going to stay with and which one will allow them to depart. The split can have a detrimental effects in the scope of family. On a much larger spectrum, the cosmic church has been slammed with the atrocity of trying to place its posture in the correct position for the birth of this great man-child.

The entire world is waiting in expectation for the birth of gods Spiritual Children. There is a cosmic commotion under going in the earth realm just before the true sons (daughters included) of God are unveiled. According to Romans 8:19, the bible says, "For the earnest expectation of the creature waiteth for the manifestation of the sons of God."   This serious aspect of the manifestation will have an unimaginable impact on this world because of the anticipation Gods spiritual children. The rocks and depths of the earth will literally be gasping and groaning because of the cataclysmic labor spasm's that the earth will be enduring. There is a great level of excitement for both natural father and mother to be excited at the birth of their child during the discourse of the pregnancy.

Even though our creator is infinite in his disposition, there is an even a greater anticipation of a cosmic birth of a Army of Man-Child that is coming forth. This manchild shall be likened to old famous television show where a friendly Ghost that carried a kind and gentle spirit. Even among his peers, this pleasant figure was known as a friendly spirit(ghost). This larger than life presence was full of kindness with not a dose of evil. The spiritual analysis will not be in the same sentiments because a spiritual application to the birthing spiritual sons will not be compared to the natural birth of the human children. Although both aspects of child birth stems from the hand and

41

authority of God, there is an extreme difference in the scope of its purpose and intent. The birth rate of natural children is booming at such a staggering and alarming rate. In light of the natural birth rate soaring, the spiritual birth rate has stagnated to the mode of the remnant. Because the confusing notion that religion grants you access to God, there is a myriad of people that have not made a connection with true God nor have they turned to the right frequency.

The dull senses of those who only been introduced to God but never took the time to develop an intimate relationship with him. The truth behind a signals never connecting or those who were connected have now become disconnected, This is a perplexing condition in that very little spiritual growth is occurring with natural children. The false expectation of natural children growing spiritually in arena is determined by the spiritual acclimation to word of God. Although the Devil given the appropriate label as the Father of lies, there is ever increasing offspring of a demonic lineage called the Children of Disobedience. The connotation of sonship works in the demonic arena as well. The dramatic impact of those who choose to work for the devil will learn that they have been tricked. This futile deception will cause many to realize that they have lost their birth right to the devil. Aside from the many souls who became dull to hearing the true and living God, they will spend eternity regretting their choice to follow the human directives.

Because he has caused too many to disobey the word of God, they have become idle in their efforts and allowed the enemy to gain access. Part of their program with many church minded individuals, they refuse to become sons of God and opened themselves up to being sons of the devil. The dispensing of the word of God without wisdom can sometimes hinder the growth of the work of the true kingdom. Children can only be truly nurtured when they are being feed the proper food designed to build them up to be healthy and wealthy in the spirit of righteousness. Religion has allowed many to abort their destiny primarily because they have been feed counterfeit food without realizing the tainted ingredients. There is a remnant child that has an insatiable desire to know HIM and to be conformed to His death that they might also be partakers of His resurrection. This come out of the box type of example are those who know by the spirit that there is a way out of this life and that is through a very real death. This death is relegated to self by way of the cross. They have not believed the lie that we are delivered from death by the cross of Jesus Christ, but unto death. Moreover, they have part in the first resurrection, being blessed and holy. However, the second death has no power over them. The bible says in Revelations 12:1-9, " And there appeared a great wonder in heaven; a woman clothed with the sun, and the moon under her feet, and upon her head a crown of twelve stars: And she being with child cried, travailing in birth, and pained to be delivered. And there appeared another wonder in heaven; and behold a great red dragon, having seven heads and ten horns, and seven crowns upon his heads. And his tail drew the third part of the stars of heaven, and did cast them to the earth: and the dragon stood before the woman which was ready to be delivered, for to devour her child as soon as it was born.   And she brought forth a man child, who was to rule all nations with a rod of iron: and her child was caught up unto God, and to his throne.   And the woman fled into the wilderness, where she hath a place prepared of God, that they should feed her there a thousand two hundred and threescore days.

And there was war in heaven: Michael and his angels fought against the dragon; and the dragon fought and his angels, And prevailed not; neither was their place found any more in heaven.   And the great dragon was cast out, that old serpent, called the

Devil, and Satan, which deceiveth the whole world: he was cast out into the earth, and his angels were cast out with him. John, the revelator, has given a recap of the future as if it was present for him to review. This was an effort of God to get apostle john mind armed and dangerous for the deeds of the enemy against the church. The woman revealing in Revelations 12 Chapter is actually a true version of a virgin Church.   Out of which, God will bring forth a Man-child remnant. In verse 1, the English word woman is translated as woman is the Greek word "gune", which means a woman referenced as a wife. The woman appears to be symbolic of the church as a collective entity noted primarily as the bride of Christ.

The virgin perspective in this day and age is certainly an interesting connotation. To think of a Virgin Church, one that has not known a man. This is one in whom the incorruptible seed of Christ, rather than the seed of man's ideology or carnality. The Great Harlot is also mentioned in the bible and her efforts are extremely diabolical. The bible says in Isaiah 5:14"Therefore hell hath enlarged herself and opened her mouth without measure: and their glory, and their multitude, and their pompe, and he that rejoiceth; shall descend into it." The profit is alluding the children of disobedience shall descend into this pit. In order to understand disobedience in a greater light, we must first under the significance of purpose. As Children of light, we serve the purpose of being sons of light. Our purpose stems is to glorify the father and serve as an extended light of him in the world. A life without purpose is no less wasteful than living life and abusing purpose. So many Christian have satisfied the appetite of Satan because they fail to embrace their purpose. When children are ignorant to their purpose, they run from correction right into destruction or a path to destruction.

Spiritual Parents, those who struggle with guidance or proper training, misuse or abuse those under their rule. Fear grips their heart and they forsake accountability in having proper authority in their lives for the sake of purpose testing. While many will adapt to this attitude, the end result will be a counter-productive & non purposed relationship. Many people have missed their purpose for failure to embrace their sonship responsibilities. The destruction of sonship is not in the individual but it is in the seed. This is the exact reason why satan has been after the seed. If satan does not get the seed, he is slick enough to cause damage to the seed while it is in the wound. Keep in mind that sickness of the devil. The bible said in Matthew 19:12, "For there are some eunuchs, which were born from their mother's womb: and there are some eunuchs which were made eunuchs of men: and there be eunuchs, which have made themselves eunuchs for the kingdom of heaven's sake. He that is able to receive it, let him receive it.

The true nature of Son can be assessed with its ability to reproduce as the seed progenitor. Sonship is threatened tremendously with this new breeding and sexual deviation of the homosexual agenda. The Greek word for sonship is huithesia. This word is made up of huios, meaning son and thesia, meaning placing. This word is used by Apostle Paul to infer the notion that we were formerly strangers and have not only become citizens but sons of God who are being transformed into His image by partaking of his divine life. The term "Huiothesia" relates to both the act and result of being made sons. It refers to the act of our being saved to become citizens and the result of our becoming sons of God in the divine life. Being naturally impotent for procreative sex, some men were historically categorized as being gay. However, the minority of gay men, were referred to as born eunuchs. The definition of a eunuch may also include a man or woman incapable for marriage, not sexually attracted to women or unwilling to marry a woman.

The word Eunuch, in the New Testament, is derived from the Greek word Eunouchos, eun, for bed and echein, to keep. The eunuch is literally a keeper of the bed. The term Eunouchizo literally means to castrate a man. In other words, a man's testicles were crushed or ruptured to the point of being inoperative. Without testicles, a man is incapable of producing sperm and therefore incapable of procreation. Sometimes, the penis is removed in the sense of emasculating the man from having any reminder of his inability to have sex. It is quite clear that all eunuchs were not castrated. The teaching on predestination is a power piece of information that carries the stigma of being revelation. A notice has been granted and it reveals who is predestined. It can only be one of two groups: the saved or the lost. Apostle Paul identifies the children of God as the object of being predestinated. God did not predestinate anyone to be saved, but this teaches he predestinated something for those who are already saved. What did God predestinate for Christians? The scriptures are pure and simple. The Christians are predestined unto the adoption of Children.

When we trust Christ as our Savior, we become His children: "But as many as received him, to them gave them power to become the sons. According to John 12:36"" we examine the context and find that the Lord urged on those whom he instilled to have faith in the light that they might become "sons of light." This reference here is more positional than relational. In other words, the sons is defined as Teknon, meaning –a child of God, even to them that believeth on his name." According to 1 John 4:9-10, the Apostle states, "In this was manifested the love of God toward us, because that God sent his only begotten Son into the world, that we might live through him. Herein is love, not that we loved God, but that he loved us, and send his Son to be the propitiation for our sins." Many Christians celebrate the love he shown us through the birth and life of

Jesus Christ. The distinction used between the two words teknon and huious can be perplexing in its use to define the type of son that exist. The results can be explained in bible says in Galatians 3:26,"For ye are all Sons of God, through faith in Christ Jesus" and again in Galatians 4:6,7"And because ye are Sons, God hath sent forth the Spirit of his Sons into your hearts, crying Abba Father. Wherefore thou art no more a servant, but a son; and if a son, then an heir of God through Christ;" Now we are under the gospel umbrella, we are no longer under the servitude of the law, but upon our believing in Christ, become the sons of God; we are thereupon accepted of him, and adopted by him; and, being sons, we are also heirs of God, and entitled to the heavenly inheritance.

CHAPTER 4
THE REVELENCY OF PRESENT TRUTH
It's in the Blood

As death comes, it gives an indication that the race of life is over. According to Ecclesiastes 9:11, "The race is not given to the swift nor the strong but he who endures until the end? Why? It is in the blood of Jesus Christ. Somehow the sentiments of winning does not seem to matter unless we have obtained the crown of righteousness. It is very easy to point to one simple scripture as the answer to all our problems.

In Matthew 6:33 the bible says, "But seek ye first the Kingdom of God, and his righteousness; and all these things shall be added unto you." However, we must do more than seek it we must embrace it.

It is obvious that theology has infiltrated in the church in such a way that we have to ascertain every conceivable intervention as if there is something new under the sun. Theology, in some circles, has become so preeminent that some embrace it more than the word of God. However, there some people that only attend Seminary or Bible College is to learn so that they redefine the context of the word to give it different meanings than the giver of the word intended. The bible has been translated and transliterated in such a fashion by scholars or theologians that the average person would literally think that this was part of the original text.

Every writer contributed in such a fashion in accordance to the grace in which they operated. In a matter of speaking, we can look at Apostle Paul's life. Paul was from tarsus and he grew up hating the church. Furthermore, Paul was a persecutor against those who were believers. Paul actually witnessed the stoning of Stephen. In the discourse of Paul, we find that he taught at the school at the school of tyrannous. Until Paul had his road of Damascus experience, he was an enemy of God. Paul was very studious and presented an exceptional appeal to those outsiders that were of aware of his intelligence.

Paul spent a great deal of time at the feet of Gameliel, a great philosopher of the day. Most modern day believers think that the English translation of the bible is the language that Jesus spoke. As such, the average Christian does not have the capability to decipher the languages in which Jesus spoke fluently (Aramaic, Hebrew and Greek). Let the readers not fool themselves to think that some of these writers have not slanted the bible in such a way to illustrate their beliefs. Some view the kingdom of heaven as a social club with no order. However, there needs to be a clear declaration that God has an army that will not break rank. We have order that is not manmade. Can you gain access to God without Jesus Christ?

Can you get saved unless the holy spirit draws you? While some have come to erroneous conclusion, the Word of God has emphatically denied that you can. Kingdom Order has always been around and shall always remain in place. The problem is that the inhabitants of the kingdom or those who have had the ability to access failed to stay in their posture of purpose. In other words, we have some who have failed to occupy their assignment and allow the enemy to gain access. There is a simple message that the members of the church needs to understand. Those who desire to know God need to plug into the Kingdom Agenda and try not to avoid it.

History has proven that inserting human intervention in the process has definitely caused many to abandon their post because they had no clarity and no full understanding. Furthermore, they had no one to go to that could give them better understanding. The dangers that occur when you reach out for someone based on human logic or reasoning is that a creature is trying to comprehend information without the correct interpretation. In spiritual matters, it is far greater to get in the arena with someone who has a daily walk with God and one who takes careful consideration and activation of their prayer life. However, life is much better when the cord of righteous or the spiritual biblical cord is plugged in to Jesus.

While truth has always been relevant, there has been a paradigm shift in the atmosphere. The skin of religion has abdicated from truth but they fail to get rid of this dead skin. Though many will shun religion, we must understand the significance in which is plays. According to James 1:27, the bible says, "Pure religion and undefiled before God and the father is this, To visit the fatherless and widows in their affliction, and keep himself unspotted from the world." On the other hand, there is a sect of demons that will take a portion of truth to facilitate their demonic agenda. Therefore, it is important for everyone to understand the need to build a relationship with God personally.

This tactic will disarmed the devils intent in its intent to mislead the masses. It is more important to build a relationship with the one source who has all the answers. There is a new energetic force in the atmosphere when seeks present truth through the sincere meat of truth. As the church enters into an awakening of this new found freedom, there is a tendency to regress towards past patterns. Instead of pressing into a new dimension, there is a continual backsliding that has taken affect. Why do believers have a tendency to look over their shoulder? The notion has prompted many to believe that there is some resilience towards a luring curiosity with the nature of sin.

What affect should sin have on the believer's. When a believers steps into the full effect of righteousness, there should be a spirit of liberty in their walk. According to Genesis 19:24-27 the bible says, "Then the Lord rained upon Sodom and Gomorrah, brimstone and fire from the Lord out of heaven; And he overthrew those cities and all the plain, and all the inhabitants of the cities and that which grew upon the ground. But his wife looked back from behind him and she became a pillar of salt. Because there is a race that the all believers are in, we must keep focus and sensitive to his spirit that we don't pay attention to the enemy who is trying to run us down and run us over.

We must keep in mind that the enemy does not only want to win but he wants to destroy the opportunity us in the process of the race. As we look in the bible, the true Church is being hindered primarily due to the Pastor only model. No matter how large relative to size, there is a missing link to the puzzle when the true structure is not in place. Why is it that we can take something out of context and make it the law. Jeremiah 3:15 says, "Then I will give you shepherds after my own heart who will guide you with knowledge and understanding. Shepherds are gifts to his churches and according to his heart. The ancient and archaic view of a Shepherd is similar to the office of Pastor. However, the church has falsely misused the function without any consideration of the blue print that God has given the Church. This Old Testament was referring to a sheep in a Pasture.

This connotation is indicative of a old testament view of Sheep and a Sheep keeper. The New Testament view of a Sheep and Shepherd is the Old Testament revealed in the new with revelation of what God would be doing in terms of the Sheeps care in the sense of nurturing. In other words, all functions would serve the follow in a shepherd like care and there would be one who would assigned the mantle to feed the flock generally. However, the mind must be stretched in the New Testament to include four other gift that would also be responsible in a shepherding of the sheep. These gifts would include the Apostle, Prophet, Evangelist and Teacher. The omission of these four gifts have hindered the essence of church from the true growth spiritually speaking because the church has been hindered. Because there can be only one shepherd over a flock or fold, there is a misconception of delegated authority versus authority.

While one may hold the distinction as one function that has been in this tenets of the text as primary authority as a caretaker of the flock does not omit the notion that he is the only caretaker. The Old Testament speaks volume of the use of the prophet and it is mentioned a great deal in the New Testament. The false pattern for every church to have a Pastor Only Model is detrimental to cosmic church development. Although the Prophet is the most talked about and written of the relative to the 5 fold gifts, but they are also the same one that everyone is out to kill as well. According to Amos 3:7, the bible says, "Surely Lord God will do nothing, but he revealeth his secret unto his servants the prophets. Prophet Amos is given the church clarity on the office of the prophet as God has given it to him. The scripture gives us an assurance of the need for prophets for the church locally and cosmically.

This further reveals that God himself has declared his need for His Church to be on point for hearing what thus said the lord. The Church if fully aware that many are fearful of the prophet because of the importance he or she brings to the table. It is also important to understand this context does not imply that God does not speak to any of the other function because he does. The point for the body of Christ to comprehend is that when there is a urgency for the word or warning we must be available to hear from the sent prophet. What happened to Gods blue print? We now see that all members tend to the flock be a strategic focus has been placed on the Pastor as being in charge. The real truth is that no person is in charge because the church belongs to God. Why doesn't the church follow and implement the God given blue print?

When the question was asked to some fellow episcopate, apostles, prophets, evangelist pastors and teachers, no one could give an answer. Nevertheless, the reaction rendered a failure to understand and apply his plan. As a result, the church has followed a conventional plan. Delusion has set in so much to say that we can do it our own way and expect God to be in it. When we respond on our own understand, God get upset and brings us a Strong Delusion. Perhaps one can now explain that God has allowed us to believe what we believe. The reaction is that we are not covered in the decisions we make. God does not have to show us mercy when we follow our own plan. Now we are in trouble because the only way we can get out this mess is with strong truth. Strong truth does not come from seminary, nor bible college, nor through elite entertainers.

It come from a strong prayer life, which produces strong fruit, which produces a strong relationship which propels into the presence of God which brings forth obedience, which releases his mysteries and revelations and ultimately make our creator a happy father. Information without the inspiration of the holy ghost is tainted knowledge with no power. The body of Christ is handicapped in that we do not have highly recognized sources of learning resources such as terms inspired by the holy spirit. Although the bible is the all sufficient source, guide and blue print, the Church needs some Holy Spirit inspired aides for those need to develop their spiritual antennas. It is impossible for most writer of dictionaries that are not inspired by the mind of God. The bible says in Matthew 11:12, " And from the days of John the Baptist until now the Kingdom of Heaven suffereth violence and the violent take it by force."

The scripture has been take out of context by many to believe anyone can take anything from the creator of all. Moreover, how does one consider such a possibility. The members of the body of Christ are given responsibility to handle certain points of access. God has sanction that the inhabitants be in point and in position. While some only want be in the light of render the word on a platform, the focus has been taken off of other essential and vital task that need be done. This has no personal reflection on God. God had already delegated authority to the believers who are so busy to realize that they actually have the authority to keep the enemy out. However, because their mind is encapsulated with religion and do not understand the power they have access. In other words, the enemy has tricked many believers into giving up the authority that they possessed.

We are accountable to the purpose and plan of God. We spend too much time refuting what is in the bible. Many of modern day apostles have misunderstood their roles and understanding of the charge that has been given to them. Some of them have been given the faulty notion that they can walk in multiple functions. However, there are multiple anointing that all believers that embrace the righteous of the Lord God. Furthermore, there is an attack on office of the bishoprick primarily because some think of its role as that of the catholic church. The catholic church did not create the office of the bishop and everyone that embraces the bishoprick is not catholic. So, it is important that the church understand that there is a cosmic church. Whether you view it as the universal church or the cosmic church, we must understand that the church started with the Church of England.

Remember that the split came about because some in-house teaching that catered to Catholicism. Another frivolous discussion is the masses effort to minimize the significance of the bishop and their efforts to make them synonymous with that of an elder. While eldership is not a calling in the sense of a function, one should recognize that it is a position of maturity. A candidate for this position should be intimate with the vision, faithful in their time, talent & treasure and supporter of other leaders in the house. The elder can be a novice but a bishop can not. It should be understand that a bishop should be a seasoned elder. With Jesus being made lower than angels gives us a modern day expression of the role of episcopacy, it was modeled after angles (or angelogy) because their roles would be the same in terms of being watchmen.

Although God is the great architect that designed the plan then implemented it by stepping out of the pavilion of Glory, he came down to the earth to wrapped him-self around humanity and embraced the name of Jesus Christ as the son of the living God. Furthermore, God also activated salvation by regeneration died a terrible death for man to be regenerated and ascended to the father to sit on the right hand of the father and providing an avenue for us to be joint heirs.

CHAPTER 5
THE WALLS OF INJUSTICE

The greatest indictment of our judicial system is the continuous plight of recidivism. The conviction rate of our African American men is so high that no one cares to see if there is an injustice in the process. Black men and Black women have been victims of a system that is supposed to be blind. While many Caucasian do the same crime, it appears that the penalty does not equal that of an African American. As black men continue in a destructive plight, it appears that their children end up repeating the same pattern of criminal activity.

The affects of this pattern continues a domino affects to the demise and disintegration of the family structure. Every generation continues to fuel a plight of destruction. The mindset is being cultivated for failure and this pattern of activity leads to destruction. The criminal element has always matriculated from the mafia. The underworld appears to have obtained legendary status as the underworld enterprise that is untouchable. In other words, the mafia has system of induction which is a lifetime commitment. Gangs are a minute spin off of a mafia type of system. The apprehension of a family like life time commitment is a unique approach to family but in another sense of family structure. This breeds a strong affinity for family loyalty as a cohesive unit would desire. The lack of the father and mother invalidates the true essence of a family unit. However, the gang feeds off of a poverty mentality of the neighborhood children. Recruitment is a major ploy to display financial opportunities through criminal activities. It is believe that the mafia serves as a big brother to many diverse gangs and serves as a source of their supplies.

In Proverbs 24:2 the bible says," For their heart studieth mischief and their lips talk of mischief" King Solomon points conveys that those who intend to do evil study the efforts of those who display a mastermind expertise in the elements of criminal enterprise. These criminals types prey on individuals usually from the low to poverty level of economic depravity. The gangs primary recruiting efforts is to approach these young guys that are easily impressed with their gang paraphernalia and the opportunity to make money. Intimidation is a method that is used to force these young boys to joining the gang. Once they are jumped into family(usually implies being beaten by extreme measures of each member of the gang) to symbolize a lifetime commitment to the gang. Members are told that the only way out of the gang is by death and if some tried to leave the gang member of their family would be killed.

The bible says in Colossians 3:20, "Children obey your parents in all things, for this is well pleasing unto the Lord." The lord intended for the children to be obedient to the parents. The problem arise when the parents are poorly trained at parenting and the children end up raising themselves. The family structure has suffered tremendously with the advent of the prison systems. Many men are either dead or in prison. Consequently, these young women are left to fend for themselves and end up hooking up with someone else living the same lifestyle. This integrated family has children with different fathers who are not living a lifestyle pleasing unto the lord. There is a warped type of loves that continues to pass from generation to generation. However, this type of love is more sensual than surreal. Due to the sexual revolution, there are many men and women who have forsake the marriage vows for a perpetual roll in the hay.

Furthermore, this lifestyle does not give any assurance of an ideal family structure. In actuality, it is the exact fuel that has destroyed the tenets of marriage. In some cases, couples engage in extramarital affairs with no remorse or conscious for their mate. For whatever reason, there seems to be a strong abatement from morality. The institution of family has disintegrated so much that many do not value the foundation of marriage any more. The justification for this behavior is supposedly associated with the shortage of men. However, the real truth of the matter is that our society has lost its fear of the wrath of God.

CHAPTER 6
THE TEARS OF A BASTARD

The spirit of a bastard mentality has been lingering in the atmosphere and our society since the eons of time. There is a cry spreading in the atmosphere for sons longing for a father that they have not seen. A gap has been expanded since the days of their birth and the longing to be affirmed The slave owners were sleeping with the slaves and a child was born in the process. Even though the child was born in the conditions presented, the slave own would not stake claim to his child due to the embarrassment that would be incurred. It is unimaginable for the slave owner to stand up and declare the child as part of his family. This child would be considered the very basis of illegitimacy. In a nutshell, these children would be crowned with thorns and declared as rejected children from their true legacy.

According to Deuteronomy 23:2-5, the bible says," A bastard shall not enter into the congregation of the Lord; even to his tenth generation shall he not enter into the congregation of the lord. An Ammonite or Moabite shall not enter into the congregation of the Lord; even to their tenth generation shall they not enter into the congregation of the Lord for ever: Because they met you not with bread and with water in the way, when ye came forth out of Egypt; and because they hired against thee Balaam the son of Beor of Pethor of Mesopotamia, to curse thee. Nevertheless the Lord thy God would not hearken unto Balaam; but the Lord they God turned the curse into a blessing unto thee because the Lord thy God loved thee" The bible says in Zechariah 9:6,"And a bastard shall not dwell in Ashdod, and I will cut off the pride of the Philistines." The Old Testament perspective of a bastard was geared towards a strong legalistic view of the core of it existence.

It is revealed that God honored legitimacy and held it to the highest extreme. Anything considered in-genuine would be tagged as a bastard. For those who violate this act, it is perceived that you would be ostracized. In other words, you would not have the permission to gain entrance into the congregation of the Lord. In a spiritual expression, the Church will not allow anyone access to prostitute by way illegitimacy. As we examine closely, God has placed a serious mandate that no one will gain entrance unless they have the right posture of being an obedient son. Otherwise, the access point would be trampled through by anyone who claims legitimacy but, in reality is a bastard. The "fake it until you make it methodology" sends the wrong message as some will try to get in line to attempt to gain entrance.

Understanding the above segment of scripture as broken down from Deuteronomy of an "Old Testament" perspective, gives a ready understanding that access is given by relationship and not by religion. Religious agenda and pursuits are likened to an mirage of a door or gate that disappears because it was an illusion. In other words, the entrance point appears to be their but is a trick of the enemy because a bastard is not entitled to gain entrance. The enemy paints a picture of that gives a false sense of security but failed to give them the combination or the right key to gain access. According to Hebrew 12:8 the bible says, "But if ye be without chastisement, whereof all are partakers, then are ye bastards, and not sons."

The word of God is clear that a true son or daughter must endure chastisement as a part of development as a son.

If a Son or Daughter rejects the tenets of the process, the son or daughter is cast away to and rendered the label as a Bastard. The New Testament is based on the elements of grace which is defined as unmerited favor. This message should be understood that you have access to the provision that were made available to those in this spectrum. Many are being duped into thinking that they are entitled to sonship rights without truly understanding what is required to be a son. Furthermore, there are those who use lip service but their heart is so far from God. On occasion, there are those who try to violate the principles such as a Son trying to birth a father. There are times and there are expected times when a son exceeds a father. Make no mistake that a son cannot birth a father. This is an in balance when a son tries to birth a father. This is a spiritual violation and one that God frowns upon because the son is trying to replace the role of the father in his life. This does not negate the fact that some fathers will not be able to take their sons into the next dimension. The changing of the guard have taken affect. This is a sign of maturity of a father that knows his

limitations. Although a son is supposed to exceed his father in the Gospel, it does not mean so in the chronological since of the word. There is definite constructive endeavor the son to glean from the father through impartation of wisdom knowledge and understanding. There are different types of a son as it pertains to the New Testament. The term teknon is a greek word for son that means son figuratively where either male or female is living in glad submission (moment by moment) to our heavenly father. The submission in this case is geared towards a selected individual by the Lord to serve as your spiritual father. The term huios is geared towards son that comes from conception. In this case, A sinner comes into the kingdom and begins his journey in Christ Jesus. In other words, this is the new creature who has embraced salvation and hungry and thirsty after righteousness. This is the new born Christian child that is eager to learn more on a more frequent basis. Let us explain, there is a son that you pour into 52 weeks out of a year relative to bible study or preaching the word of God.

CHAPTER 7
THE DIABOLICAL AFFECTS OF THE GAY & LESBIAN AGENDA ON THE BIBLICAL EXPRESSION OF FAMILY!

The closet doors have opened and everyone who has had preconceived thoughts about engaging into an ungodly affair with a person of the same sex is now in the forefront. The ardent nature of this sadistic agenda has detrimental affects to family disintegration. This agenda will forever impact this nation as no other nation has ever been impacted. When the head leaders of Countries made a concerted declaration to legitimize support to legalize the rights of the gay and lesbian couples, the family institution that we know shall literally become disintegrated. Once this agenda is fully recognized, the impact on family will never be the same. For instance, a can of worms is about to be turned over in respects to the rights of gays and lesbians to be legally married and the rights to obtain children obtained through a legalized process of adoption.

This will implode with the deterioration of the family unit and children will be introduced this new redefined definition of family. The detrimental affects will contribute to the erosion of family structure. No longer will the father be able to mold their child because the child will now be conditioned to view his parents as either two males or two females. The family unit as we know it will become a crop failure due to the new definition of family. The reproduction rate of children being born could possible decrease because the sexuality of male and female will decrease. However, there could be a rare situation where a homosexual couple and lesbian couple could decide to intermingle for the sole purpose of sharing the birth of children between the set of couples. The altruistic example is a classic model crop failure when the seed cannot be reproduced after its own kind. The bible clearly talks about the every creature could be reproduced after its own kind.

According to Genesis 1:26-31 And God said, Let us make man in our image after our likeness and let them have dominion over the fish of the sea, and over the fowl of the air, and over the cattle, creeping thing that creepeth upon the earth. So God created man in his own image, in the image of God created he him, male and female created he them. And God blessed them, and God said unto them, Be fruitful, and multiple, and replenish the earth, and subdue it: and have dominion over the fish of the sea, and over the fowl of the air, and over every living thing that moveth upon the earth. And God said, Behold, I have given you every herb bearing seed, which is upon the face of all the earth, and every tree, in which is the fruit of a tree yielding seed, to you it shall be for meat.

And to every beast of the earth, and to every fowl of the air, and to everything that creepeth upon the earth, wherein there is life. I have given every green herb for meat: and it was so. And God saw everything that he had made, and behold, it was very good. And the evening and morning were the sixth day. As God rested on the Sabbath day sitting in the pavilion of Glory, he reflected on his creation. The supplication presented implied that God saw what he had done and said that it was very good. This pattern of thinking indicates that our creator was happy and satisfied with the work of his hand. While there are prognosticators that really don't care about the truth, they are either atheist or non believers that have tapped into to this new world order. The futile attempt of scientist who have been bought by the highest bidders for research funding that would assert that their idealistic findings could prove that human beings are born gay or lesbian.

While there is a great debate among human minds, God has already given the answer. While clever in intent, many homosexuals' theologians pursue efforts to destroy the legitimacy of the authentic creative pattern of marriage. For generations, our society has been trying to find a reason for the adverse spirit. Scientist have seriously been researching to disapprove through theory that a person could be born this way. In essence, a perverted agenda has been proliferated and promulgated in every conceivable arena to unleash an inoculation of the homophobic euphoria. Because creations allowed for alarming rates for birth of children, men and women were seeking pleasurable arenas that could be assessed without the risk of bringing children into the world.

Psalms 95: 7-11 says, "For he is our God, and we are the people of his pasture, and the sheep of his hand. Today if ye will hear his voice, harden not your heart as in the provocation, and as in the day of temptation in the wilderness: When your fathers tempted me, proved me, and saw my work. Forty years long was I grieved with this generation, and said, It is a people that do err in their heart, and they have not known my ways: unto whom I swear in my wrath that they should not enter into my rest. Because he is our God and has dominion over all created beings and animals, he stands in a pivotal posture. The psalmist epitomizes that He is our God, therefore it is expected that we praise him. If we don't praise him, who will if we don't. He is our creator, and author of our being. We must reverence him by kneeling before our God who made us and all the world. God is the rightful proprietor and our Savior of our blessedness. He is noted also as our founder and yet the very foundation of our existence. We are the people of his pasture and the sheep of his hand.

In the same note, there have been futile attempts of scientist and idolaters to attempt to develop theories to subjugate the minds people into thinking that God had made a mistake in creation of human beings. This agenda can be traced all the way back to the days of nimrod when he slept with his mother in law. The doorway to promiscuity and drugs widened the doorway to sexual perversion. Not to mention that there are those who have crossed the lines with animals. This naughty by sin nature has engulfed society with an extreme perversion of sex. The exploitation of sex and the continued misappropriate behaviors of previous, presidential candidates, congressman, senators, governors, mayors, lobbyists and all types of political activists, bishops, priests and church leaders.

God is extremely angry with the actions of those who continue to sin and those who try to shield sin. Furthermore, he is fueling with anger for those who justify this abominable act of sex between members of the same sex. Moreover, sin can be characterized when mankind misses the mark. Such as the case of men desiring to touch a man because they have been expose to one another in the shower of the local gym. Horror stories are continuing to evolve from the past of many in their family ancestry. The debauchery occurs in cases where a family member is raped by another member there family. Aside from the fact that incest is deplorable, the exposure to the homosexual lifestyle is conveyed in aggressive manner. This behavior is perpetuated in our prison systems because a prisoner is considered a void of rights. Because both male and female prisons condone this act of regressive aggression for inmates to have a release, there is propensity to allow this to take place as a substitute while on lock done.

The damaging effects of this behavior sometimes continue in the lives of prisoners after they are released. Once the prisoner is out of jail, he has the tendency to revisit their natural quest for a member of the opposite sex. Although this is their preference, the substitution methodology continues to encounter mental notes of their experiences with members of the same sex. This pretense causes both men and women to revisit the mental notes and exploratory search is then presented. When incest occurs between members of the same family, there is an extremely high price to pay. Historically speaking, a young lady finds herself in a bazaar circumstance after waking up from a festive occasion to find herself in bed with her uncle. Under normal circumstances, this would the epitome of a wild encounter with a pickup from a party.

However, the psychological affect's of knowing that you were so inebriated from a night of heavy drinking at a family reunion that you ended up in bed with your mother's brother. Other alarming occurrences where a person awake to find that you are in bed with your little cousin and realize that you have had sex with her can have a traumatic affects. The matters get worse when the cousin finds out that she is pregnant and decides to keep the child. While there are serious consequences in the dating and mating game, there are some family that don't care as long as you are further down the family lie such as third or fourth cousins. The family, on the other hand, is disturbed that the incident occurred.   Furthermore, they fill that the child will be a constant reminder of the incident. Look into matters where a father ends up having a baby by their natural daughters or aunts sleeping with their nephews.

So many disheartening secrets are hidden in the closets of many families that cover up the incident that is considered taboo. What about the case where a mother ends up sleeping with her son. The confusion of sexuality started many moons ago with this rebellious and perverse generation. Generational curses have been lobbying in the present atmosphere and are primarily the result of this devious behavior. As a result of this, families must hold their children to a sacred standard that a family don't intermingle sexually with members of the same family. Also, it should be a major emphasis that family should not marry and have babies because of the identical DNA. This would taint the children to the point of mental & physical

defects. However, the homosexual and lesbian don't have a mark to miss. In other words, it is simply a deviation by design.

The creator of the blueprint for both male and female has sustained in eternity. Furthermore, God never designed a blueprint for couples of the same gender to intermingle. He destroyed Sodom and Gomorrah for this same behavior. While many try to justify the mere existence of behavior,, we must avoid the notion that this is acceptable behavior. We need to lobby against such behavior and demand that this behavior is punished as a severe crime. There will always be extreme nut cases where those who support this fastidious pattern of living. Further attempts and efforts are being made to legitimize this agenda to give them further rights. This campaign is just another attempt to give rights to something that God never intended to take place.

The united states of America was built on Christian principals but now it appears that it should be categorized as being created on religious basis. Perilous times have come due to the world due to its entanglements with sin. How long is God supposed to allow this mess to continue. When will he unleash his wrath on those who don't seem to think that he will respond to them in the spirit of his love. Because all authority belongs to God, mankind has truly fallen away from the tenets of faith. Speculations indicate that the wide spread missive for the pursuit of the legalizations of gay and lesbian marriages is spawned by Hollywood and the Hollywood Activists. In spite of their wealth and influence, they have no interest in what the creator has convey because they see themselves as gods. Their money and influence is supposed to give them entitlements to change the element of historical precedence.

The wakeup call has also invaded the church coming in the extreme nature from leadership in the church to the pew members. The premise of many who have been tricked into believing this lie are starting their own churches and continuing in this lie. There are attempts by practioners to search the scriptures and try to expand the meanings of word particularly in the Hebrew, Greek and Aramaic language. While the act may be implied, it is not acceptable as a lifestyle just as multiple marriages with strange women were detested. The fact gentiles had an extremely high amount homosexual activities intermingled in the lifestyles of some of the elite inhabitants. However, just because it has been around does not mean that God endorsed the lifestyle. In the modern day militaries, the acts of homosexual activities were forbidden.

It was detested so much that any member caught in the act was literally release out of the service. There have been occurrences where individuals wanted to get out of the service so bad that they imitated the gay lifestyle in order to be released. Furthermore, there were occurrences the military changed its attitude to a more subtle approach. Don't ask and Don't tell was one of the campaigns used by the military to prevent the public debauchery of some desiring to embrace the lifestyle.

CHAPTER 8
THE DISCOURSE OF MANIPULATION & CONTROL

The spirit of manipulation & control 's origin began all way back to days of the garden, when eve was beguiled by the serpent. The matter at hand was premise by God giving authority to Adam, who then delegated instructions to his eve. The danger comes when another speaks into your ears and tricks you into questioning those instructions. Whatever the reason may or may not be, there is always a choice in the matter. Historically speaking, the course can be traced back to the days of intensified witchcraft. The subtle nature serpent is cunning, slick always conspiring to use whatever method they can to get the desire outcome they desire. Rest assure the outcome will only be beneficial to the one applying these type of tactics. The bible says in Job 14:1 "Man that is born of woman is a few days old and full of trouble."

The fallen nature of mankind is essentially affected to the point that once the child exits the womb the enemy has placed a target on the child and seeks to destroy its destiny. According to Proverbs 30:11, the bible says, "There is a generation that curseth their father, and doth not bless their mother. This generation has angered the lord because they have failed to honor their parents. When a child speaks curse words or vulgar language towards his parents, this behavior violates the core of his immutable existence. Proverbs 30:17, the bible says, "The eye that mocketh at his father and despiseth to obey his mother, the ravens of the valley shall pick it out, and the young eagles shall eat it." The above mentioned text conveys that any child that does not reverence his father or mother is cursed by God. There is a blessing when the family unit is connected on a wholesome and vibrant basis. God gave each member of the family a role to pay in which there is an expectation of honoring him through the headship of the father.

The chain of command relative of authority was never granted to Lord over family members but rather in the scope of being an ensample. Although a dictatorship type of authority was an abusive style of leadership, it was more of a control form of authority that was not from God. As a result, this type of leadership violated the members and caused them to rebel. This type of leadership is a subtle form of witchcraft and it appears that many leaders are utilizing it to the point of achieving the desired results. However, God does not grant anyone this slave oriented mentality because he wants them to adapt to a leadership style where inhabitants respond as an ensample rather than from a dictatorship style of leadership.

The bible says According to 1 Samuel 15:23, "For rebellion is as the sin of witchcraft, and stubbornness is as iniquity and idolatry" Rebellion occurs when someone rejects the authority of God or his delegated authorities in which he has established. There are many levels of legitimate authority that is often forgotten that delegated authority is the same authority handed down from the one who carries the authority. Some of the authorities are the authority of God himself, the authority of the Word of God, the Authority of the Holy Spirit (and delegated authorities such as governments, fivefold leaders, parents etc). All of these authorities are established by God and should be obeyed to the full extent. Some executive leaders must examine closely those given delegated authority as a method of abuse. It is apparent to the parishioner that some new to being in positions of authority don't quite understand nor do they handle the authority as well.

Needless to say, some given positions where delegated authorities exist need training to become affective in their performance of exercising authority. Moreover, there are major complaints that some protégées abuse delegated authority. Witchcraft is a subject that most people cringe to think about. Furthermore, the mere mentioning of the subjects brings a sense of fear for the unknown elements of the subject. The thoughts compels many to conjure up graphic images of black magic, voodoo, black pointed hats and the flying broom sticks in movies. Practicing witches, both good and bad, take every form from simple nature worship to casting spells and invoking demons. The adverse reaction of the subject propels some to respond negatively to hear about the various forms of witchcraft that they themselves may be using and not even be aware of the use. The notion of unknown use is as dangerous as the stereotypical form.

However, there is a very subtle form of witchcraft which goes unrecognized even though it is just as evil and dangerous as the stereotypical form. There are three ways where witchcraft invades our society, our churches and our homes. The access portals focus primarily on manipulation, domination and intimidation. It is also very truthful churches have been hindered because of the spirit of witchcraft. Exodus 22:18 Thou shalt not suffer a witch to live. Although the first five books are referred to as the torah or Pentateuch, it is reluctantly credited to Moses for the writings. As such, the writer of Exodus points out that a witch or one practicing witchcraft would be hard pressed for them to live. Furthermore, it also implies that the inhabitants would not allow a witch to live.

Deuteronomy 18:9-12, the bible says, "When thou art come into the land which the Lord thy God giveth thee, thou shalt not learn to do after the abominations of those nations. There shall not be found among you any one that maketh his son or his daughter to pass through the fire, or that useth divination, or an observer of times, or an enchanter, or a witch, or a charmer, or a consulter with familiar spirits, or a wizard, or a necromancer. For all that do these things are an abomination unto the Lord: and because of these abominations the Lord thy God both drive them out from before thee." The writer informs the reader of the desperate agenda of witchcraft and the occult to use every available tactic of demonic agenda to pollute the core of the divine plan of the God of truth. Furthermore, Apostle Paul says in Galatians

5:19-20 Now the works of the flesh are manifest, which are these adultery, fornication, uncleanness, lasciviousness, idolatry, witchcraft, hatred, variance, emulations, wrath, strife, seditions, heresies.

Although Satan functions in the atmosphere, he primarily targets the areas that appease the flesh. All of the above mentioned things that Paul imputed in scripture, hinders the spirit man and causes bitterness to set in. He capitalizes on the physical dimension of the flesh to feed its appetite and to cause it to be continuously feed by those sinful things that upset God. As a result, the spirit man becomes dull and the ability to communicate with God is further stretched out. Consequently, the plan of the devil has been implemented to steal, kill and destroy the destiny of as many willing vessels that fall prey to the devils master plan. In a nutshell, Satan has started a plan to alter and control the minds of our children to through recruitment initiatives. Once a child is seduced by the devils carefully designed plan, the devil is enabled to control their minds at a very early age.

Satan's diabolical scheme is to infuse witchcraft into the educational portal via required reading for students in public schools. They're mission is to indoctrinate children with witchcraft as a soft approach to expanding an off shoot of religion. While witchcraft is being taught, pushed and required reading by public schools all across the nation, the subtle approach is a public relations effort to change the negative connotation & image of witchcraft. There is a method to this madness to push America further into darkness and to move the true and living God out of the equation. In other words, this is an all out duel between darkness and light. While the Bible is ostracized from all public schools, children are learning at a very early age the evils of witchcraft. Some of the materials pushed, promoted, published and promulgated into the hands of all public school children.

Witchcraft is a distinct initiative seeking alliances from any spiritual source other than God. The primary portal used in society stems from horoscopes, astrology, tarot cards, sorcery, séances, psychics, palm reading, spiritualism, fortune telling, necromancy, yoga, new age meditation, Chinese zodiacs, burning candles, chants, spells, charms, the rosary and icon bracelets. The trend in society has created an oscillation from darkness and light. There seems to be a pull from the light instead of pulling people into the light. While darkness has had its place in Gods design, it was never intended compete with darkness. When God created day and night, it was designed to give keep them separated from one another. According to Genesis 1:4, the bible says, "And God saw the light, that it was good: and God divided the light from the darkness. Isaiah 45:7 I make light and create darkness: I make peace, and create evil: I the Lord do all these things.

It is amazing to see the deception of witchcraft in its power pursuit. However, scripture supports that God created evil for his purpose and his pursuits. Now evil desires to destroy the very source that created it. The devil is aware that he cannot destroy the source that created him. However, he is determined to cause a commotion of those who he may deceive. This agenda has been implemented inside the walls of the Church. This action precipitates the notion that the wheat and the tare have always coexisted. Witchcraft is evil to the core and utilizes strategic measures of setting up corporations that publishes all the books to public school children. Drugs and alcohol are gateways into the demonic spirit world. Those who engage in substance abuse are sending invitations to demons to infiltrate and control their minds often drug abuse is intentionally used in witchcraft to make contact with demons.

The devil uses witchcraft to control those who are seeking for something but not understanding how the spiritual dimension works. If you implement biblical principles, you will find that they work in both dimensions. The nature of manipulation occurs at every level of the family. When a child want to do something, the first endeavor is to go to their mother as a point of contact. The second phase of this method of operation is to go to their father and play their agenda off that one parent had already agreed. In actuality, the children just manipulated their parents playing one against the other. Husbands manipulate their wives as an effort to go out with the guys with an occasional business meeting at the golf course or basketball game.

Wives, on the other hand, manipulate the husbands in terms of intimacy until they get the desired result that is wanted. The family dynamics play a vital role in family formation and structure. With one parent missing, this element of functioning is lost due to the obvious nature of the discourse. A bastard or orphan loses out of this element because of the sins of his parents. The time has come for the parents who make choices that affect their children psychological development. When a child is stained with the notion that they don't have legitimacy, it gives the notion that love is not in the equation. The value system has eroded due to the poor choices of a one night stand or casual engagement of a sexual encounter. In other words, the world does not care of the outcome of the sexual encounter just as long as they have some form of contraceptives. The fact that children are left in a extremely depressed condition of life for not to having the true essence of legitimacy. Acceptance of the times is not a prerequisite for a child to lose the quality of life. However, the core of a man's ego has prevented him from being an effective provider, effective husband and effective father.

CHAPTER 9
KNOW THEM THAT LABOR AMONG YOU
Diffusing the bastard mentality!

We are living in the days where many have associated their lives with old adages of our predecessors. One that comes to mind is the proof is in the pudding. The pudding would not be authentic without the process of integrating the various ingredients into a bowl for stirring. In I Thessalonians 5:12 Apostle Paul states, "And we beseech you, bretheren, to know them which labour among you is unto the Lord, and admonish you;" In the natural world, it would not be productive for a son to grow up without spending time with his father. The progressive journey is a discourse for children to have quality time with their parents. There are certain intangibles to a child learn from their mother and their father. When both parties don't participate in the first 20 years of life, the child loses out on the rites of passage. However, there are some good parents that raise their children in the non-traditional setting.

In other word, some have reared their children without being married and some have raised them in spite of a divorce. Because the Church has an urgency to become the body of Christ, there is a propensity to over-look certain intangibles such as sin. It appears that there is a continuous declaration of the soon return of the Lord and Savior Jesus Christ. However, the church remains in a cocoon like posture instead of blossoming like a beautiful butterfly. Furthermore, the church must understand that the process is mandatory. This is the part where everything gets twisted. In order to have access to the provisions and benefits, you must position yourself in the posture of a son. It is legitimacy as a Son which is the nature that grants us access to Righteousness.

Sonship gives every believer the access granted to the benefits of righteousness. The opposite of a son is a bastard. There is a drastic difference in the mental makeup of a bastard and a son. Although they appear to be identical, the slope tilts download to the negative. A bastard is unholy, untrustworthy, ungrateful and unruly. The bastard child will not only the affects of being legitimate but also will lack the capacity to embrace the love which they lack due to their poor family structure or not structure at all. In other words, a bastard child does not have a cohesive unit family to shape his life. The atmosphere of the legitimate child is conducive with love, nurture and positive affirmation. When fathers are missing in action, there are some key ingredients in the development of future generations.

There are many wounded children limping and bruised due to displaced and /or absentee fathers. For the bastard child, the father bring a needed element into the Childs life. It is important for fathers to think of the welfare of the Child when the desire to enter into marriage. Many relationships are fruitless in this regard because the sole basis of most relationship's are fueled only by sex. There should be a bigger purpose in marriage than just sex. As a matter of fact, the term sex is a world term that should be recognized as love making. The bible says in I Timothy 1:9-11, "Knowing this, that the Law is not made for a Righteous man, but for the lawless and disobedient, for unholy and profane,

for murders of fathers and murders of mothers for manslayers.

For whoremonger of them who defile themselves with mankind, for men stealers, for liars for perjured persons, and if there be any other thing that is contrary to sound doctrine." The spirit of religion have invaded society so much to say that most are struggling with identifying truth. As a result, there is an attitude that an imposture has a falsified entitlement. This form gives a hollow perspective of righteousness and a falsified form of religion that caters to the religion. This is the case when those who fail to plug into God and only wants to know about him. It is high time that that true remnant of God will endeavor to stand up. The office of the bishop has come under great scrutiny. Although the office has made many valuable contributions to external Church management, there is a great deal of uncertainty as to who can or cannot occupy this administrative position. On one hand, it appears that the office of the bishop has been place into a position unwarranted by God.

Instead, the position has operated in authority that God never intended. All across the continent, there are splits that have occurred because some of the individuals have violated serious sins. On the other hand, there are cases where an individual exercises their God given vision and the call on their lives. While it is true the some sins should warrant the person to step down or abdicated due to moral deviation. The religious sector is quick to label one a heretic when one deviates from what they feel is the edict of times. In other words, the religious sector has set a precedent for church diplomacy. Instead of allowing constituents to flow in the vision God has given them, they rather label you detrimental to their vision. In actuality, these organizations are likened to the nicolaitans that Jesus firmly stated he hated. However, it is the doctrine that Jesus hated rather than the nicolaitans themselves.

Part of the problem that Jesus had with the nicolaitans is that they held similar beliefs to doctrine of balaam, who taught balak to put a stumblingblock before the children of Israel, to eat things sacrificed to idols, and to commit sexual immorality. The nicolaitans were a type of pagan religious system that followed the false teachings and allowed themselves to crept into the church, disguised themselves as followers of Christ, who confessed to be His ministers and servants but lead the people astray. Some would characterize the office of the Bishoprick has a very similar cast of people slip in through the side door of episcopacy with people who try to do right thing in disguise but really are designed to lead astray. Apostle Paul knew what was in store for the church as Ephesus and shall also be in store for the church today.

He knew then and it is apparent now that a great threat would arise from among the members inside the church as oppose to outside. This is

Satan's great strategies whereas he would much rather transform himself as an angel of light or as a wolf in sheep's clothing. This way he can come in undetected, and do everything he can to introduce enough leaven to the whole lump. We are fully aware of the parable of the wheat and tares, that not everyone who looks the part of a true Christian is actually about the Fathers business. A portal has opened to the extent that many come in the name or title of a Bishop but, they have misunderstood the purpose of the office. The method in which some have accessed this office is truly incomprehensible. In a way this agenda fueled by men who rather give it to men with impure motives, improper qualification or who never comprehended proper protocol or understanding of episcopacy.

There are men are so desperate to expand their vision from other countries that they grant unqualified individuals improper authority to men on a quest for titles. Furthermore, the bastardization of the title bishoprick and the conveyance of historical apostolic succession has become a mainstay for individuals expand their effort for personal gain. The quest for legitimate Apostolic Succession is unmerited by some of these individuals because they were never committed to the ones who consecrated them to the office of bishop. Some of these individuals are angered because one organization in which they were apart overlooked them for promotion to the office of the bishop. They become so bitter and upset that you likened them with a pack of dogs on a chain. The parity of a pack of dogs on a chain is an excellent example of what the bishoprick has become.

There is a reason that dogs are put on a leash or chain. Every dog is given a certain area of coverage in order to roam. The office of the Bishoprick has a similar pattern. (Although I am not calling bishops dogs, I am using this a model to illustrate a point of view) Some dogs get so angry and they break the leash or chain and embarks onto a new journey. The same sentiments of a son the breaks covenant with its leader before time or run from one organization to another organization in effort to gain access. Each of these situations carry a decree of bitterness. In a nutshell, the bishoprick has become a portal for men to treat it like a pack of dogs. This response is due to a need to be promoted based on their lack of understanding or training. When of the office regains its splendor for the intended purpose of serving as a watchmen over a delegated sphere of influence.

This will given each bishop a clear understanding that you are appointed to do an assignment as a delegated area of influence. In others word, you cannot be a self bishop and serve like a bastard. Furthermore, we have the insidious individuals creating their own sense of legitimacy without ever being trained in the episcopacy. This reproduction system has only spewed out illegitimate episcopates. In actuality, they are not qualified to be labeled episcopates. Some of these so called bishop carry the title but have no clue to the integrity of the office. There is a fastidious need for the church to realign in order to retrain these individuals to have a better understanding. This is a serious problem in the collegial system of episcopacy that does not keep a data system to warn them of these new found predators.

These individuals are only angry and out to prove that they can become bigger and better than the other organization than the organization they once were previously apart. These individuals only desire to promote their bitter agenda and parade around their new found mission of expanding the kingdom with unqualified individuals who have never physically spent time with candidates. It is apparent that Satan has infiltrated the Church in the realm of leadership. If you cut the head off, you can take the body and do as you will. The moral is that these men were never trained or effective in the lower ranks that they saw fit to recreate something new without seeking God for

forgiveness. When an agenda is centered around bitterness and competition, the foundation is weak and the crack shall surely implode.

Anytime and organism or organization is given authority under this pretense, there is an underlying current for the organization to fall on its face. Apostle Peter states in I Peter 1:10,"Wherefore the rather, bretheren, give diligence to make your calling and election sure: For if ye do these things, ye shall never fall:" In other words, Peter is telling all who read to give heed, to recognized, to acknowledge, to embrace and press in to the calling and election for which you were called. Further, he is giving those who read this scripture that focus is necessary to do what's necessary to learn all about your calling or election. Once you have done this very thing, he is ready to inoculate you with his anointing to do greater works that he has prescribed for your life. On the same note, there is another type of son in Christendom that is currently on the rise. The orphan is a son that is a leader of a Church that does not have nor desire to have any spiritual parents. This is a problem that goes undetected in some church circles.

However, the premise is that sonship is a required connection portal to have relationship with God without having a relationship with physical spiritual parents in the Lord. The bible says in Ephesians 6:1, "Children obey your parents in the Lord for this is right." This scripture reinforces the notion that there is a great need for spiritual parents in the local church. Unfortunately, everyone parent is not considered an authentic parent in the lord. Without having a relationship with God, there is no connection to warrant the status of sonship. When the set leaders, husband and wife, are in covenant with church members, there is a transitioning from members to children in the lord.

This subject matter is not accepted in most circles because some believe you forfeit the status as an orphan the moment you accept Jesus Christ as your lord and savior. God is considered every believers father and they become his children. While the above mentioned point is marginally correct, God has set the precedent for the set leaders of every local church as the Parents in the Lord. The problem with this conception is that everyone who believes in God by the letter, but has not accepted Jesus Christ as the only begotten son of the father. In other words, Jesus becomes the literal key to the Kingdom of God. In accordance to I John 4:2-3 the bible says, "By this you know the Spirit of God: every spirit that confesses that Jesus Christ has come in the flesh is from God; and every spirit that does not confess Jesus is not from God; and this is the spirit of the antichrist, of which you have heard that is coming, and now it is already in the World."

This is infallible proof that Jesus Christ is the only access point where man must accept Jesus Christ as the Son of the Living God. Since all creations is part of his plan and purpose, we must understand that the fallen nature in which we were born in is fatal and deceptive. The fall of Adam propelled man in a sinfield state of being. As a result, the posture of many would more than likely place us in a bastard or orphan state of being. The focus should be on legitimacy of sonship for which both bastards and orphan must exercise in order to be reconciled to a loving father once they accept Jesus Christ as Lord and Savior. However, the alternative is to allow Satan to take over the church as a bastard or orphan and literally allow the church to become a "synagogue of Satan"

CHAPTER 10
PARENTING IN REBELLIOUS TIMES

Parenthetically speaking, God is the ultimate source of love. He displays his love to his creation, to his nature and most of all to his children. There are five essential Greek words for love in eros, philia, agape, storge. Initially, eros is the root word of erotica that is initially felt for a person with contemplation as it becomes an appreciation of the beauty within a person. It could be stretched to imply that a physical attraction as a necessary part of love. Therefore, it would be faceous to say or to imply that platonic love to a person epitomizes that there is no physical attraction. Philia is characterized as a type of love for a friends, family and community. Agape simply means, "I love you" from the creator to his creation. It is best illustrated between Jesus Christ and the disciples. In other words, this type of love is given in spite of the circumstances.

It is a type of self sacrificing and it is rendered in the sense of giving love to all both friend and enemy. Matthew 22:39 the bible say, "And the second is like unto it, You shall love your neighbor as yourself" and in John 15:12 the bible says, " This is my commandment, that you love one another as I have loved you." Agapeo is an extended type of love from agape that best illustrated by God our creator as the one who loves but has nothing to do about the one being loved. The lack of input from the recipient makes it possible for us to love our enemies even though we may not like them or the situation that they may have put us in. Nevertheless, this type of love is expected by the believers but is often misunderstood by nonbelievers because the recipient does not understand the essence of agape. Storge is characterized as a type of love that is a natural affection which is best described as a love from a parent to their child. This particular term is used to denote intimacy between a husband & wife to have intercourse.

In the same sense of rebelliousness particular in regards to the sexual revolution, there are many singles and married individuals the enjoy the marital benefits of intimacy but fear the opportunity of becoming parent. Many of the feelings are characterize by generational curses that have been levied in a downward spiral. There is an intensity of failing in the role as a parent especially when society has difficult times in the process of parenting. The learning curve has expanded with great fear in failing as a parent. Sometimes these feelings are the result of abusive and gross negligence on the parent of parents. The saddest thing in the world is for children to be born into a family that did not want them. They were a result of a sexual relationship that went bad. Many times women feel that they can keep a man if they have a baby. On the contrary, there are many cases a bomb blew up in their face and a new reality has proven to be a major error. While it is true that parenting in the United States is likened to the ok corral, there seems to be a light at the end of the tunnel. The synergy level of fear has increased to deal of abortions, or displaced babies either found in the garbage or found on some ones porch. Nevertheless, it is critical when a parent can abort a child or try to have some form of early termination of the pregnancy. Some prospective parents become so depressed with the fear of a having a child that they become manic depression. While there are multitudes of single parents that have done a marvelous job of raising their children, the children suffer because the parent is working multiple jobs to make ends meet.

Walking on the wild side always looks and feels good, the lifestyle that comes with it would put the mothers in dangerous situations and warrant investigations with Child protection agencies. While the norm of raising children as a single parent has always leaned towards the women, there are some dynamite men who have stepped up to the plate and taken their rightful place in their children's life as the custodial parent. Although every case is different, there are times when the mother may be incarcerated, loss by death or separated by extensive drug habits. The psychological deterrents are increasing at an alarming rate with Children reproducing a endless cycle of kids raising kids. When we take a closure look, it is astounding to find that there are thousands of children being born to literally babies that have become early mothers by proxy of sexual intercourse without protection.

While some girls through playing with dolls become obsessed with having a baby, they don't fully understand that a real baby cannot be place on a shelf or in a treasure chest when they get tired.   Furthermore, these young girls are having babies without fully understanding of the cost of child rearing and the loss of their freedom of childhood. While the rate is alarming, many grand mothers and fathers end up carrying the load because the children feel like they have been placed in a trap. Instead of learning from this early motherhood, the young girls are so eager for independence that they get of the system of public aid. They move into local housing thinking that the fun has begun to latter find the difficulties of surviving on public assistance. These young inexperienced girls become prey to the local dope dealers who flash a little cash and drive the fancy cars.

The young girls are extremely attractive and attracted to the money and the bad boy image. The efforts to defuse this behavior is perpetuated by poor family structure and usually means that there is only one parent at home. The children are sometimes left unattended because the parent cannot afford an adequate baby sitter. Some of the young ladies become so stressed with life challenges that they get into the drug game. Not only do they put their life in danger, but they also place the children in an intense situation because of the high risk of a drug raid or robbery for competing drug gangs.   While there are endless sources of negative elements in society, the main ingredient is that these young girls are looking for the wrong thing in the wrong places. These young girls make it worse because now they have been taught how to dress to get a man's attention.

Once they get his attention, they have to provide avenues to keep him. However, this young man will keep several woman on his key chain and let them know that they are all his girls. There is no shame and the women feel a need to share him just to get a piece of him and an occasional portion of his money. Satan has made is so appealing to the eyes that the incumbent do not realize that they both are seducing each other. Some people enjoy engaging in intimacy but fear the out -come of having children. The absent ingredient is faith in the word of God. Proverbs 9:10 says "The fear of the Lord is the beginning of wisdom: and the knowledge of the Holy One is understanding. Many don't realize that the all powerful and sufficient one should be feared by one who created he them. Whenever the creature tries to figure out the creator in terms of relevance and authority, there is a profound comprehension in the process of the beginning and ending. All authority and power are in the hands of God as he delegates his righteousness through his creation.

Psalm 111:10 says, "The fear of the Lord is the beginning of wisdom: a good understanding have all they that do his commandments: his praise endures forever. The writer of psalms indicates the fear of the lord as in respect or reverence for our creator and his laws(word), his will, and his government(his delegated leaders). Furthermore, the creature is so in awe of God that there is a fear of offending him. The writer's emphasis is placed on an upright heart for the incumbent to do what is right by his word and by his delegated authority. This authority is implied in the church and in the home.

However, the instructions have been conveyed but often times they do not implemented. The spiritual parents of the local church carry authority from God to convey his will through his word. The parents of every home carry authority from God as a delegated authority over their children. Many great atrocities occur when parental authority is perceived to be misused and abused because the parents have not been trained and developed thoroughly. It is clear and concise that the problem is monumental because babies are literally raising babies. Young mothers have played Russian roulette in the game of securing man. However, it appears that a perpetual cycle has been purported as the game of life begins. Just like the ball is placed in the spindle of the roulette, the girls placed their life on the outcome of the spindle as an effort to attempt to establish a relationship.

Majority of these relationships end up with an undesired pregnancy or some play ground portal for a casual sexual relationship. The same pattern is exhibited in the church. Sexual sins have become the norm in the pulpits and there does not seem to be any Godly fear with regard to their actions. Spiritual fathers have crossed the lines to misuse & abuse their Godly authority to engage in sexual affairs with their spiritual daughters. Spiritual Mothers have also crossed the lines with their spiritual sons to actively engage in extra-marital relationships. Spiritual Incest have crept into the church and into our society. These grievous & pernicious patterns of activity have assisted in maligning of the integrity of the local family structure and the church. Aside from the wheat and the tare coexisting in the church, the leaders of the church have fallen into apostasy. It appears that the leader of the church have fallen on deaf ears especially as it relates to sin.

Apparently, the leaders have started engaging into acts that would indicate that the presence of the Lord no longer exists in these churches that have lowered their standards as it pertains to the word of God. The church is full of babies and it is apparent that there is no one willing to serve as a true spiritual father. The concept of spiritual father has not fully been embraced nor does it appear that the masses desire to get a full dose of fatherhood. Mankind continues to push themselves away from God as they continue to commit sin without any fear of retribution. Improper teaching in certainly apart of the equation and it appears to be no one else to willing to serve as the father to these children. Many men will lay down with the women but will getup, take a bath and go home. In other words, the women were good enough to sleep with but not good enough to marry.

It is time for men to search their hearts and minds to determine if hell is truly a place that they desire to go. God is not happy with all these babies who carry the stigma of being bastard. He never intended for babies to be born outside of wedlock. These children did not ask to come into this world under the banner of being illegitimacy. God never intended for the world to be inhabited with some many children that have no legacy, no home and no family. This dastard deed is for spiritual parents is to prevent them from feeling the affect's of their life without their mother or father. In some cases where both parents are deceased, there is another type son that is referred to as an orphan. The orphan is defined as a son with no parents. This unwarranted classification is noted as a child that does not desires to have any parents. On the contrary, every child deserves to have loving parents to comfort, nurture and to protect.

The sentiments should be carried over in the respect of church leadership. Every visionary should have spiritual parents to speak into their lives, to comfort, to nurture and to protect. While this phenomena is truly missing in the body of Christ, it is the missing ingredient for these hired pastors to embrace. Because parenting is considered a season piece of the equation, it is vital because it is also the foundation of early development.   If parent of leaders can truly examine themselves, they would truly understand the need to assist their children by sharing their development with another parent. The same sentiments should be used for spiritual parent as well. When we realize that there are limitations of the family influence, we must prepared to seek help from another.

No one person can assist you in full maturity of your life without handing the batons off to another leader. that can help their child reach full maturity. Unlike, the natural parents would only allow someone to baby sit their child. This is more in line of progressive revelation that the natural parents may not comprehend but will benefit their child in monumental ways. For instance, many of the older generation never attended college and fail at the possibility of help their children with their homework assignment. It is quite possible the some parents would attempt to assist their children but will convey to their child that they need to reach out to someone who has the same skill level. The whole concept is to find someone who can help take their child to the next dimension or next level.

This is why spiritual parents have to evaluate their spiritual children and locate other options to assist their child when in shifting to another level. True parents will welcome the new parents in the shift because the sole objective is for the children to reach his destiny. Because there is a strong objection to spiritual parenting in this society, there is a strong tendency to embrace the notion that they don't need any spiritual parents. The greatest indictment in this notion is that many embrace the bastard and orphan mentality without realizing that God made other people to be their parents. Why would God go to the extent to make Abraham a father of many nation's. There is a clear and concise example the fatherhood extends beyond natural understanding of the home front. The choice comes down to do you desire to reach the plateau that God has in store for you. Too many churches have placed their leadership in the hands of seminary graduates.

The problem with present student graduates is that they are so use to instructors (professors) and forsake the true fathers that God has in store. As a result, this mentality could cause some to miss out on the blessing that God has in store for them. According to 1 Corinthian 4:15 the bible says, "We have ten thousand instructors in Christ, yet not many fathers; for in Christ Jesus I have begotten you through the gospel." Release the orphan and bastard mentality and embrace the parents God has in store for you.

CHAPTER 11
CALL NO MAN FATHER

Fatherhood is a noteworthy subject that is most often a thought in the mind of many individuals that may have experienced child birth. It is one thing to help birth a child and another thing to be in the nurturing stages of a child life. For this reason, fatherhood is likened to an endangered specie. The discrepancy with fatherhood is that there many men who will claim to be a father but in actuality they are sperm donors. In other words, men will donate his sperm in the sense of a participation of the process.

There are some serious cases where men have accumulated more than 15 children and he is not married to any of the mothers. The atrocity of this matter is contingent of the readers view of this situation. Even though this is a staggering number of children, does this male have a right to be called a father. In every case, there is different reason but the same response.

Men think that it is something to brag about when they inform their buddies and family as to how many children they have amassed. Now that state agencies have had to intervene for the sake of child support, the lips begin to stammer when the incumbent is informed by the courts of the amount of child support that he is expected to pay. It takes more than time spent in the bed to make a baby than to be a real father. More importantly, a real father will take the responsibility to be in their child's life on permanent basis. According to Proverbs 4:1, the writer Solomon declares in the bible says," Hear, you children, the instruction of a father, and attend to know understanding." When a child is born through marriage, this child

is on a discourse that is designed by the master plan and will of God. Furthermore, we must declare that God never intended for children to be born outside of marriage.

This tainted endeavor was designed and implemented in the minds of the people by Satan. The bible says in Matthew 23:9, "And call no man your father upon the earth: for one is your father, which is in Heaven. The enemy has attempted to halt a child in a restrictive sense not to refer to his biological father as a father. However, the true essence of this text was speaking more in terms of giving reference to another as a Father more than the Father in Heaven which created everyone and everything. In other words, this text offers us clear instruction that no bible teacher or instructor would ever refer to themselves as the source but on the contrary, they would refer to God as the source and the power and truth. Although the term "father" is not something that is referred to by many, there is a sense to call another man by his last name as a reference to honor and respect.

Parents would never allow their children to refer to any adult by their first name. It is truly a sign of disrespect when a child refers to an adult by their first name. One of the first responsibilities of a father is to train them in the area of protocol. Furthermore, a man who does not live with his children would not be able to monitor their children effectively. Our heavenly father never intended for children to be raised by one parent as the custodial. He designed the institution of marriage for couple to walk as one and the children to be a blessing to the union. Sometimes, the decree of divorce is a hindrance because of the covenant that was once established has now been severed. This new trend in our society, especially in the church, has perpetuated a domino effect. The bible is clear in its dissemination of truth. There is an erroneous doctrine where men and women in the faith declare that they have no need of a Spiritual Father, Mother or Covering. This is clearly a doctrine of devils because everyone must have some level of accountability with another. Unfortunately, some spiritual fathers may have died and left their sons or daughters feeling like they just cannot replace him. Although new schism have come forth, it is a trick of the enemy to be on an island by yourself. Timothy and Titus were referred by Apostle Paul as Sons of the Faith. Needless to say, this endorses clearly that apostles have a covering as well. The problem is not just a covering but praying for someone who can carry you or point you to the next dimension. In other words, the covering concept should be opened up to shed more light as to who can cover another.

While most might not agree, there must be a grace upon certain individuals life to be able to cover someone. One of the misfortunes in this life is that there are some people who are not able to cover nor impart into the lives of others who carry a seed that the leader cannot help reproduce. It is important to note that some preachers may be seasoned but may not carry the grace the reproduce the seed in your life. On another note, we must also realize that some children may be in our lives for a season as a temporary covering until the one who carries the ability to cause the seed in your life to truly manifest. Although a common term in the world but not in the bible, the term "Dad" is used by a married man with serious biblical values and children as a result of marriage. In Ephesians 6:4, the bible says, "And you Fathers, provoke not your children to wrath: but bring them up in the nurture and admonition of the lord.

Apostle Paul admonishes fathers to raise their children in love rather than hatred. There are multitudes of people who are bitter at their children who were a result a relationship that was either failed by the affair or the result of a divorce. Sometimes, the parent will blame the child and brew hatred as a result of it. However, the children should be raised purely by the world of God and live in ways of the lord. The divine order in the home should be the foundation of the family structure. It begins with the husband because God made him the head. According to Colossians 3:19, the bible says, "Husbands, love your wives, and be not bitter against them." The sacrifice always begins at the upper portion of the family structure. In Colossians 3:18 the bible says, "wives, submit yourselves unto your own husbands, as it is fit in the lord." Apostle Paul gives instruction to the women that they must submit to their own husbands.

Whereas women are considered the weaker vessel, it important that they remain focus and submit to their own husbands. Moreover, this endeavor will allow women to keep their eyes off of another couples accomplishments and focus on the potential achievement of her own family. There is always a propensity to access value of another families accomplishment's as oppose to the value of their own accomplishments. This nature to compete is not necessarily a positive notion in family corridors because they can be counter-productive. The pride of life is an area where many fall into a trap especially in the entertainment and sports arena. The gateway to demonic influence give way to Hollywood and professional sports.

Many of the actors and athletes do not have plans for marriage so they live a wild life. One of the greatest athletes in the world became infected with the aide's virus. Some athletes are continuously living double lives and fueling a double jeopardy of an outlandish divorce settlement. The agenda of many of the candidates are fueled by financial security. The amazing thing is that the incumbents of the messy divorce's ends up in some form of reality show where the women or men can make more money and expose their lives even the more. In Every industry, there are groupies that hang around so that they can get their fangs into one or more of these celebrities. These celebrities are furthermore opened to opportunities to engage in more activities that could be damaging to their careers. Some of the groupie's only desire is to get pregnant to have their babies and secure financial independence.

The sentiments are shared in the entertainment industry where co-stars are having affairs that end up destroying a married by added a child to the equation. This costly behavior apparently gives way to the actors who find themselves attracted to one another after they have engaged into a passionate scene of a script. There are multitudes of door way opening when these succumb to their appetites which were open via a role from a script. Majority of the actors are open to a door way of Satan. The movie industry has been a monumental access portal for Satan to gain entrance through unbelief and disobedience. The entertain industry sooths the door way because many of actors and actress have other religious beliefs that are contrary to the bible. However, there are some who have operated in the entertainment industry and have held their religious convictions during their stay.

However, there is a strong desire to see those who can close all demonic portals that hinder their walk with Jesus Christ. The life style of the actors, actresses and sports professional inhibit a counterproductive journey that does not make Jesus Christ the head of their life. Religion shall always be a pseudo for righteousness in the sense of a cosmetic diversion for the real thing. Now that religion has tried to slip through the portal with homosexuality, adultery and fornication (sex with different partners), this pattern has violated the Genesis plan in which God created - one woman and one man becoming one before one God. This plan was created to protect and bless mankind. Now the whole world is messed up and much of it has to do with the fact that illicit sexual acts give legal access to demons to come into the earth (and our individual lives) to create havoc, curses, soul ties, addiction's, strongholds of physical, mental and spiritual character.

This is why Satan works overtime to over-stimulate society with sex in media, movies etc. and increase the perversion on earth. The devil efforts to get more people involved in his "plan of destruction rather than the original plan" of God. As a result, Satan can access and develop a stronger foothold in the earth. Satan has infiltrated the institution of marriage through an access portal that enables the enemy to gain even more ground. Whenever the enemy gains any ground, there is a need to rebuke the enemy. True spiritual authority can only be effective when the vessels used are submitted to almighty Gods Authority. It appears that some use marriage purely as a gateway for financial security. This person is usually called a gold digger. There is landslide expression when people get married for all the wrong reasons or for reasons that only benefit one party of the marriage.

When a wealthy person prepares for marriage, they ponder in uncertainty whether or not the person has genuine love for them or for the amount of wealth he has accumulated. In any case such as this, one has to wonder if the marriage will be done with the genuine motives. Normally, there are signs that illuminate when one candidate is not sure if the person truly loves them for better or for worse. Because of the laws of the land, many wealthy people take the necessary precaution and request their mate to sign a prenuptial agreement. The premise of this agreement is a legally binding contract that declares that their mate is not able to access their wealth if a divorce decree is granted. This agreement may have some conditions that may include a severance package or it could imply that you brought nothing in the marriage so you are not entitled to anything. Because of the dangerous times we are in, some people take the necessary steps to prevent someone from using the institution of marriage as a plot to gain wealth due to marital decree.

In some states, the spouse can clean a man out just because they were married. Some states grant many women marital assets by dividing the estate proportionately. The world has come to grips with this method to test whether or not the person really loves them. Some men place contingencies in their prenuptial that imply that as long as you live together as husband and wife, you are entitled to certain luxury benefits in the lifestyle that they have become accustomed. If there are any children involved, the children would stay with the father as custodial parent. There are also some conditions that indicate that the children will have certain financial benefits with a lucrative financial trust that will not be accessible to the child until they reach a certain age.

The Christian community would condone this kind of behavior because they take the marital vows seriously. Each person committing to the vows of marriage, says for richer or for poor, for better or for worse in their marital vows before God. The sugar daddy is a label given to a much older man who finds himself in a relationship with a much younger woman. This relationship is characterized as companionship. This relationship could be based on pure company of the younger lady. Often times, this relationship is precipitated by sex for money. The older man is more generous with his finances and the young lady fancies the notion that the older man will take care of her.

This person serves as a father figure to her and rightfully so, he feels a need take care of her as a custodial father. The twist in this scenario is that sex could play a vital role for both of their needs. The God Father is a character that has taken on a god complex that is usually centered around the mob where he is the chief figure in the underworld of Crime. Furthermore, he is highly honored and revered by the other mob bosses. The crime families are notorious on one hand but highly visible in churches every Sunday. The God father complex has given him a mirage of authority that is estimated to be so powerful and respected by public officials, police officers, union officials, politicians just to name a few. It could be that in this case that the father knows what is best. No one can take the place of the true and living God who is the only Father who has all power and authority that no man could ever amass or embrace.

This is the true reason that the scripture was fearful to call any man father because they would try to portray they had the authority and power that belong only to the true omnipotent and omniscient God. As long as man can reverence the true father, there is no problem with man being referred to as a type of father who points to the true father in heaven as the ultimate source of power and authority.

CHAPTER 12
THE KRYPTONITE OF FATHERHOOD

Apostle Paul says in I Corinthians 13:11, "When I was a child, I spake as child, I understand as a child but when I became a man, I put away childish things." There is propensity to look at this text to see if men do as the word instructs. This text examines the plight of children as they progress into manhood. The journey implies that during the transition period from a child to an adult that there should be a sign of maturity. It is truly safe to assume that Apostle Paul was instructing the reader that those who claim to be men had put away childish things. Also, there are some men that become selfish because they do not have any morals when it comes to doing the right thing. The connotation for this implication means that they have been placed inside a treasure chest. If the mindset continues to oscillates towards the treasure chest that is full of nuances of their life, this implied that certain things had been put away as an indication that they were attempting to move into maturity.

Furthermore, this would give the wife an assertion that access would only be opened if it were a matter of a father using them to be a rites of passage to their young boys. However, this challenge is presented as an empowerment endeavor for men to press forward in their pursuit of manhood and allow childhood antics to stay locked into the treasure chest. Now, there is nothing wrong with reminiscing about past mistakes that a father made in order to help mold the character of their children. One of the key roles of father is to give guidance so that the child can make a well informed decision. If more fathers could give their sons and daughters a hand up, this would be invaluable the child's future development as the child passes into adulthood.

The invaluable lessons could prevent the child from make the same mistakes their father made. Although this could potential be very invaluable, this is not a preventive measure for stopping the child from making any mistakes. The primary reason for this endeavor to share with their child so that they could be transparent with their child. This would allow the father to share in some of the mistakes he made as an adolescent. Furthermore, it is those fond memories that fathers share with their sons as a legacy of tradition which is being passed down to the son. Every father has some lessons in life that he can share with his son about transitioning from childhood into adulthood. These lessons could come in the form of experiences that they faced as a child with similar circumstances.

When a man fails to grown up or mature, there is a paralysis that hinders his mindset and the mindset of future generations. Many men fall into this trap because of fear to share the truth about the reasons for failure. There a multitudes of men who have lived off of a dream to play a professional sport but failed to hit the books and get a good education. Part of the fallacy in their mindset is conditioned by their local surrounding of where they were reared. Because of the need to assist their parents, many made bad decision and turned professional. In effort to make the big leagues, many had struggles that prevented them from making the dream a reality. However, the bubble burst for some many because the reality has set in. Now, they have to pick up the pieces of their life and find a new direction to follow in order to survive. The decision to decommit to the class room studies has limited them to a particular type of job.

Many fail to see the significance of school and the school work that they over looked while looking to shoot straight for the stars. Life is about choices and responsibilities for the poor decisions that were made recklessly. Instead of hitting to books hard to get a degree, many of the athletes live on the premise of an illusion of grandeur. In other words, their egos are so large and society had given them so much hype to the point that they are better than what the scouts had perceived. On draft day, they found out that their stock were devalued or mentioned minimally if at all. To make matters worse, they do not get very many offers to sign as an undrafted rookie. With all of this unexpected jargon going on, they got offers to go overseas as a special project in the developmental league to refine their skill-set. As the light begins to dim, some of them come back home to face reality that they just did not meet the criteria to make it to the big leagues.

Instead of the big money playing in the professional league, they find a job washing dishes at a local restaurant or cleaning the very schools that they played. Apostle Paul states in Romans 15:4, "For whatsoever things were written aforetime were written for our learning, that we through patience and comfort of the scriptures might have hope."The missing ingredient of these individuals is the lack of faith in the scriptures and the God who wrote them. In most of these cases, the individuals developed an ego that was much bigger than their ability to play at the next level. The lack of humility allowed them to put the cart before the horse. While each of these individuals was given a level of talent, they never sought to give God any praise or glory for the talent in which he had given them. Pride set in and they felt no need to give him honor nor did they give him the time, talent or treasure.

Because of the lack of preparation fundamentally or academically, they were embraced of the returned home to be among their peers. The dangers of the hype allowed these young men to over project their ability to go to the next level. Many of these guys barely went to school, and their grades were given to them just so they could be eligible to play. With a newly instituted and regulate program called proposition 48, the net began to squeeze tighter because so many athletes were allowed to receive scholarships that we not academically prepared for college. Through the maze and variation of proposition derived programs, each talented student could receive the scholarship but had to sit out the first year of school to work on their grades.

Some of the intricate factors considered for college included class room grades, core class grades, ACT or SAT scores. In order to protect the kids from jumping straight into the pros, these students had to play one year of college. However, some of these athletes already had children coming into college. The burden of playing sports, hitting the books, enjoying college life and providing some sort of financial support to their girl friend and child have to be extremely stressful. The pressure for college athletes is not an icing of cake. These students are legally bound to attend classes, workout session, training sessions, tutoring session when necessary and during the off season of their sport odd jobs to make ends meet. While this may be the extreme case, many athletes who really don't care how many women they slept with or how many babies that they have in each city they travel. Unfortunately, these fathers end up losing more than all the wealth they thought they desired.

These individuals become part of the equation as an absentee father who missed the opportunity to be a dad. While this issue is much bigger than just sports figure, this issue could rest with movie stars, businessmen, Professors, Accountants, Doctors, Lawyers, preachers or any number of successful career advocates. When the child grows up and ask questions about their fathers, the mothers tell the story of the relationship. These children are saddened that their father was so consumed with the dream of playing professional sports but did not have time to be their father. Some of these children only desire the benefits of sharing time with their father. Unfortunately, some of these fathers never grow up to be men. When will these children put away childish things and become men.

One day, the son will approach this man and ask him the million dollar question. How come you did not include me in your life? What did I do for you not to want me? Can you explain to me why I did not matter to you? Why didn't you fight to be with me? The plethora of questions could be endless because this will be on the minds of the fathers who have nothing to live for now that the dream is over. As the child wakes up, he soon realized that life has continued, his body has aged and he has nothing to show forth in his journey. This man has awakened from a dream that continued into adulthood. The problem is that he is still doing childish things. He failed the test to put away foolish things. Some think that your age is an indicator of your maturity into manhood. But, the truth of the matter is that some men are still children and never matured into manhood. The very thing that allowed you to remain in a child like state of being is the kryptonite that prevented children to become men.

SUMMARY

In summary, every child disserves their rights to have legitimacy and to have a fun field life as a part of their journey from a child into manhood. When a child is exposed to biblical principles by mother and father, there is a balancing act on the scale of life. The importance of marriage and the opportunity to wake up or go to sleep knowing that mom and dad are in the other room. It does matter if mom and dad are married as oppose to living in the same house. The true identity of family is truly epitomized when it done under the auspices of holy matrimony. The legitimacy of the family is substantiated when Jesus Christ is the foundation for the marriage. Let us destroy the legacy of the Bastard and the Orphan as we strive to walk in the love of God who can take the sting out of the nature of a bastard. Thank you father God for being the greatest father of all.

A REFLECTION FOR THE AUTHOR

It was the authors intent to call forth all fathers to reclaim their rightful place into their children's lives. We must return, repent and restore the rights that were given to us before God levied the curse. The only remedy to detonate the effects of the curse of repentance and truth. We need men all over the world to tear down the stigma of the bastard and give our children their legitimacy that was robbed from them in the beginning. In order for the affects to be eradicated, there is a need for the fathers to build a relationship with Jesus Christ.

The writer presented evidence of the after effects of a bastard. According to Deuteronomy 23:2, the bible says, "A bastard shall not enter into the congregation of the Lord; even to his tenth generation shall he not enter into the Congregation of the Lord.

www.ingramcontent.com/pod-product-compliance
Lightning Source LLC
LaVergne TN
LVHW021451080426
835509LV00018B/2239